X/S

EDWARD KAMAU BRATHWAITE

X/Self

Oxford   New York
OXFORD UNIVERSITY PRESS
1987

Oxford University Press, Walton Street, Oxford OX2 6DP

Oxford New York Toronto
Delhi Bombay Calcutta Madras Karachi
Petaling Jaya Singapore Hong Kong Tokyo
Nairobi Dar es Salaam Cape Town
Melbourne Auckland

and associated companies in
Beirut Berlin Ibadan Nicosia

Oxford is a trade mark of Oxford University Press

British Library Cataloguing in Publication Data

Brathwaite, Edward Kamau
X/Self.
I. Title
811   PR9265.9.B7
ISBN 0-19-281987-9

Library of Congress Cataloging-in-Publication Data
Brathwaite, Edward Kamau.
X/self.
Bibliography: p.
I. Title.
PR9230.9.B68X7 1987   811   86-23915
ISBN 0-19-281987-9 (pbk.)

Set by Rowland Phototypesetting Ltd.
Printed in Great Britain by
J. W. Arrowsmith Ltd., Bristol

CONTENTS

V

An then suddenly so
widdout rhyme
widdout reason

you crops start to die
you cant even see the sun in the sky;
an suddenly so, without rhyme,

without reason, all you hope gone
ev'rything look like it comin out wrong.
Why is dat? What it mean?

For Mexican, with all my love

I

Letter from Roma

Thick portly women
with meaty assurance

have come here to my study

with missives from the emperor
electing me 'the governor of the thirteen provinces'

they have brought me a white
tunic of fine embroidered dragons

embraced with silver threads and tight tan

fitted pantaloons brown coonskin boots lined with lambs
wool and golden buckles furnished from the armour of my father

they have drawn cool pearl
grey gloves above my wrists

and with a bearskin hat topped with two
peacock feathers of cerulean blue they will improve the zoo

i am pleased that they should do these things
the conqueror my father would have grinned to see me in this

gallant guise his wife my mother would have smiled

through hot and burnished eyes to see her son become the sir
vant of the sacred emperor

but for their sakes and also to confess

because i love the guile of velvet and the plumes of pride
because i like to point commands and know that slaves will yes
because i long to smile and pirouette among the ladies

toast master at their banquets brawl in the lords back room
i let these women in

these women are the messengers of court the widow
dowagers the sly important mothers nurses to the king

who suckle him with secrets feed him slim

and supply the palace with all its leaky scandals
on their huge social bosoms rear and career the fates

of admirals and cliques
their plump perspiring cheeks have to be kissed by the asp

iring courtier

and be cajoled by every artist in the town into a hiss
ing beauty

on state occasions they will sit
apart in ostrich pharaohed canopies sep.

arate like critics
but in a fine position to observe the goings-on

who
was with

who

which deco
2 the sub

loo
tenant of the land

ship wore

how dear and dandy was the new
ambassadore

a pity that he didn't know the
bitch

was such a

sure!

and always planning as they fan their cheeks
who should be next conquistador

who will replace ole tamboerlaine
how soon the next bloodbath

so standing where i am upon my study mat
i watch them watch me with their piggy eyes

someone must trust his hand into the sweetpea bush
to blind the hornet and the rattlesnake

they think it might as well be me: a withered student
propping all night among these falling leaves
of books i can no longer read

i am the chosen bridge/groom they will light
with these tall blooms and compliments
to the tormenting dead

already while i wait my head goes giddy
their fat bejewelled fingers clammy hands
that search me out: tieing a tassel: tapping a link

make my blood itch: the mad blood fricates rise and rough
me as they rub against the
ridges of my vest

and when they raise their arms
the cologne waters of their last ablutions
mingle with the sticky wet and foetid vapours rising

from their charms: i clutch

the secretaire: knocking my discarded tunic to the floor
they laugh: their slow eyes glittering
greedy points of sapphire cutting at my pride

when all is ship
shape as it should be and they have slipped
the rings of office into place. my left ear pierced. a tiny

censer of perfume
a little obelisk of arabian gold hung dangling down
and idealized my cheeks again with pale phoenician puff

these women leave me

wadelling through my study door on greasy thighs
and huffing up their nostrils in their fat exertions
and i know now that what they go to say will make the candid

emperor my uncle laugh out loud
and when the glinting terrorists i go to ride against
begin to hear of it: i see them smile

coiling new shining cobras among the paddy fields

the conqueror my father's wife would hang her head confused
if she were here to see her son so fopped
and peacock'd for a circumstance

for which he was incompotent
and all the squelchy women
of the palace

know it

II

Salt

Rome burns
and our slavery begins

herod herodotus the tablets of moses are broken
the soft spoken

whips are uncoiled on the rhine on the rhone on the tiber
severus the unlocked tiger of wounds lacerate me

syracuse is a white rumble of desolation
the train drifts slowly here slowly

like the last lava of the volcano

nicosia smells of garlic and greeks
nikarios and ships bells and the grey tunic
of guns

there is no sun
in alexandria date palms and gourds
in the desert the islamic whordes are arising

scimitar saracen saladin my companions of the curved cross
the bosphorus awaits cannon tennyson
salonaika and the dead sea shells of the dardanelles

the stones of venice are cold

gondolas of king arthur's nights bring the jews in at evening
with soft wet step and shadows under their eyes
they have sold othello the moor for a pillar of salt

but the tribes the tribes the tribes are arising like mulled
wine

there are no olives left in lebanon
in the camp of the visigoths vercingetorix the arvernin creole

chieftain

has met che has met kismet has met young doctor castro
liberators are being guillotined from heaven

along the ho chi minh trail

caesars daughter is pompeys wife
what a wedding what a knife

julia my long gowned token television star

the sky has been cut into square blue holes in the ruined
colosseum
and there are no laws left no glitter no guilt

aaron hammurabi dracon

sparks of horses hooves make stars along the adriatic
the franks
pour into gaul into the lime trees of saul

hadrians wall
known only to jordie goats
and the precursors of the textile industry

o bordeaux o engine driving manchester eternal winter of niagara
falls

where is the iron of hercules the balanced apple of hesperides
atalanta atalanta my dappled darlin dahta
which races have you run to seed to spoor to speechless broken

spider?

rotundas topple the architecture of your corner
o little jack horner the colossus of rhodes
the pretorian garden and jupiter up the capitol

wall

they are destroyed by leaks eked out by whispers
the beguiles
of women and the new among the nancy intellects

3

who brought from carthage the sister of the desert
aloes and muslim aphrodisiacs white silk billowing in the harm

attan

who brought from nubia the memory of youth
naphthali adder and tutankhammens tombs

who dripped that nightshade lead into the veins
of aesop and alcmar and the so-called coarse-grained socrates

who half blinded homer with hemlock
brought his four legg:ed ships to rome

who planted the sun in copernicus
gold of unbalanced clusters

who figured the atoms empire out
who exploded its trigger

under the dome of st peter

the slaves groan
cerements of bone
and alabaster

rises in hellelluia

4

and in the desert
john

in the desert
cry of krystos

in the desert
implacable mohammet

their messages create missiles
prisons systems the howl of horsemen across the flattened world

5

rome burns
and our slavery begins

vultures wheel over kiev over khybir over ayub khan
vultures wheel over the ganges over the crossed swords of shiva

over the dead garden of mahatma gandhi

vultures wheel over the styx over maggiore over the ice
brick blocks of the alphs

over the frozen body of el cid   .   of lidless legba l'ouverture
over corbusier over the red

flags of marseilles and the radio television francaise

over the charnel of d-day and the white cliffs of dover
over the scheldt over the cool whistles of fiords over thor over

gaar over baldur

they wheel high over the desert over tripoli and tunis over
the head waters of the nile over

chad over timbuctu over lagos over ile ife over ibadan and the
fat markets of abomey

they wheel far out over the whisper of hirohito over the ch'in
dynasty

over the manichures over the ming over the grey humpbacked wall
of the mangles

6

cry babylon
galileo galilei is free

far out across the lake of galilee
the aztecs wheel around their painted whips

Edge of the desert

I

In the deep south
away from the ner

vous pomme
granite coast

we observed trails
pathways like wires

from the air
it was a liquid voiceless
pepperpoint of fires across the darkened continent

marrakesh messaoud edjebi atshan

oases of the coconut
that cut green skull and helmet in my hand
milk fruit virgins of lamenting water emerging out of shadow

i hear the fall of carthage
tumbrils around the gardens of the ports of spain
coir mats against the skin dirt crawling like this desert

into flash more fires the dying crawling
in their living garbage
the lepers walking fully clothed across the tundril land
the kettle singing sieve to time too sand to save the world

fort gouraud lake faguibini garrotted heroes of the foreign
legion timbuctu
the sun rides ahead of the carnival to kano

emirs spears scimitars rock
shimmer fulani goat milk lapping the gourd
the heat in the palm of your bridle the sweet running down
with your blue

2

rome burns

the desert multiplies its drought into this child
whose only drying water is his pools of singing eyes there
underneath the long thin camel shanks of what will be forever noon

chad sinks
and forest trees crash down
there is a crack within the uttar stone of ethiopia
watch where the mediterranean sea comes seeking through

where cleopat unmummied peachskin coloured chick
floating to harvest in her berth of hippo milk
loves antony her sallow liver of the olive groves
the widowed nipples of her breasts pout north to slavery

Julia

In that long gown supple marble plinth capital column superb
balustrade of breasts
i see where caesars young mulatto sister will parade her
formidable chic

we know she knows no hens
ice
picks perhaps
the blue cubes placid in the crusted frost electric gourd

but claudius her husband never is at home
at grapetime tv supper time or when she takes her pills
and now there is that terracing of worry underneath her eyes
that all the dark mascara of the evenings cannot hide

would you have married ali when he was mohammet of the blow
by blow? would you have made it on the late late
cosby show? you would sign i know to appear with apollo
but could you boogie boogie on down

with tina and toots at apollo?

for a long time now there have been rumours at court
montgomery bus boycott stars falling on alabama
now we are the world will the new posse take you along?

there are no water marks along the edges of the desert
there is no corn there is no salt there is no prophet
a chip of metal surfaces at sagres on a sea of mercury

and follows follows follows follows where the vultures ride

my dreams have been piled into silence
like the leaves plied up under your tree
clear pitiless glass an ocean of haze and horizon

mirages mirages mirages mirrors re
calling good television times
palm trees in their plots in miami

there are no shadows everywhere

under the flat rocks syphilis with glare
black scorpios angry at my being here

the owl has lost her eyes with staring
the nightingale her voice too far from stars

what news from gaza o my countrymen
is john the baptist baptist yet?

there are no shadows everywhere

but in the centre of the storm
spinning icicle out of heat
of light lost in the wolves

in the memory of night fish
at the roots of lovely water
spark/le of fin into finitive music

alto flute tenor viol da gambia

his feet wish fish these reeds tomorrow
for then there would be water not chimera

his hands reach out towards the rushes for the child
still locked to sleep and cradled in the river

by his silk wet sister nephtha pharaoh's daughter

when the crow rings
he will have sighted atlas and the mountains of the moon

Nix

This caesar has a nose like richard nix
and walks about the appian way in old newspapers
time raps him wrong but he is warm
behind the bars of his atomic furnace

look where he crosses the rubicon in a cloud of rust
riding to town on his red catallac
look how he rapes the sabine drum majorettes
and offers vinegar instead of coca cola to the pretorian guard

but somebody has thrown rocks into the dust closet where his
armours are
cong john brown the nervii jack
johnson knocks him out

and all this caesar knows
is bad for the pax for the laws for the eagles
for the bread and the circus and the state religion and the
household gods

is there a soothesayer in the house?
is there a sweet-tooth puller?
is there a bankrupt bunker?

and so the ides of march
the day of pigs
sauteurs and diem biem phu

default defines defeat defects the system

et tu brute?

the whole wide world of wheels
wheels in my head like capitol

michelangelo has not curved marble
for it yet but you can bet

he will

giotto has not yet painted
his white house tower

rose white yet
but you can bet

he will

and satans mighty wings droop to the stony ground that is not
bread

for when the lake
dead

the rockies
will rock

when the dome
break

is like fall

ing

Phalos

And since that day at addis at actium at kumas
our women have forshook their herbs forshorn their naked saviours

the ragged dirt yards where they lived sister to sister wife
by wife
pestelling down a thunder of yam at babalawo's command

they have straightened their nostrils where they would flare
o julia o baby g

painted their eyelids blue like helen o like the prow/ess
of greek ships
like on the darkened dardanelles of v-strike bombers

fire of their breasts in brassieres they pour their palmwine
into harrods crystal

their steatopygia from calabash and yabba into designer jeans
they have stilletto tipped & toed on gucci heels from accompong

their mother

and now they cannot buttock down to hearth or cooking pot
to tuntum achar eddoes

they dream of rubenstein of vogue and guinevere at camelot
at arthurs fogey castle

they have become wise foolish virgins credit card viragoes
yehudi burns them into violins of sacramental fire

like eschak mescak and abednegro

The fapal state machine

I

Hannibals elephants were typical   mo
bile armour   the
knight on his charger wrapped in his sword

general patton and archbishop rommel   tri
umphant in their tanks   the softest centre
is always surrounded by helots by pawns by hedgehogs and by

phalanxes

in rome
god and his armies have become identified with each other
each sees the others amber'd face

rivets and clanks obey certain immutable laws
though nobody opens their mouth to say what they are what they
mean

claudius mine uncle has become divine
charlemagne had other problems
aix-la-chapelle was not on the tiber and his timbered halls were

not

made of stone   he
could become   caesar
but the pope   demanded his god/head   O

kay?

the barbarians lurking in marsh and forest
sasabonsam nibelung troll druid celtic locksman
the state machine cannot function on mist on mystery on magic

and on char
nival and carpenters and fishermen and dialect and walking on the
water

there must be city centres surrounded by cut stone stockades of
metal morals
murals of high deals that march the man

scape like police   big
multi-storied buildings with theat. ricals
to them   wide

steps for clattering down   white lions   greek
urns of innocence   chipped cheeky cherubs   metallic
flatters to the president   green tidal gardens that conform

to plan   chinese or stone or persian   perfume or zodiac

there must be priests well trained all alabaster and intense
ten years at least behind bars of their books lawyers likewise
the spare parts of their youth well spent in teasing tort

and tortured argument   peak headed generals
black hearted patches on their other eye   cyclopsian commanders
who eat maps and know the treacherous route to gall and warm and

jaguar

2

above all
sense of order

consider law
itself and for

itself itself

and then the precepts
that are crooked within

itself itself

say whether they be good or bad and if they come from god
and if from god whether from god from god or through an

agency like angels or from some other agency or does it come
from god at all

if not from god

from wince since there is god and only god and always was and is
and ever shall be

seen?

he (yes)
he lives in heaven (yes)

women will not compute out where the eagle flies
and where the eagle flies there is his world and eyes

there is no other world or worlds or word for world or eyes

3
this word is

writ
ten soon and known as holy writ and later holly

wrood

be
stowed on all for all for ever or on some

select/elect

how/man how/many few how/furious
how/black how/brown how/byzantine
how/ever fat how/bit into the apple how incurious

19

for if the laws be crook. ed
if pathways to the palace where/in
justice/es are not made strait

there will be
buildings rushing upwards on a scream of sand

there will be
always highways littered with the red of dogs

there will be
cinemas of buchenwald lit with sarcophagi of gas

there will be
laden vessels in the night ablaze with spice and jewels

on an iceberg

there will be
armies bleeding in their bivouacks and living off the rattas

of the land

there will be
changeling priests to chant you pop instead of litany

there will be
would be healers festering like mangoes at the bottom of the bag

scholars whose minds will smile like cheese
their ragged theses straggeling to please the new demonsthenes

4

without this apparat this parthenon
this fapal state machine

these sleepless shears
these lookout crucifixions on the cliff

there will be
scabbard legions clashing in the night

there will be
riots fires insurrections nkrumah's heedless statue broken down

the universal sun eclipsed by man and time and chaos
ships slipping past the pillows of hesperides

to where there should have been no wind no water hoof of
world no word

towards
where marco polo could not walk

towards
young caliban howling for his tongue

towards
algonquin pontiac discovering his arrows were on fire

towards
tupac amaru ii

towards
my heart at wounded knee

towards
red tacky bleeding in the west

where canefields are laid out black green sick yellow greed dry
man song bone and seed whose every sugar sweet will be
your mothers rape and shame and love vine strangling the wall

so that these christofaring ships now safely rocking harbour
will have the throats of their anchors cut
their pilots hooked

and marinate
their rosaries and choker coral necklaces thrown overboard
to the dog

sharks

and it is dark dark dark
in paradiso
in dante's villa of valhalla

in this chess checkered chapel of our hell

Song Charlemagne

I

Le jour est clair et le soleil luisant

roland est mort god has taken his armour to heaven
roland est mort god has taken his armour to heaven

roncesvalles roncesvalles roncesvalles

pas de piste pas de sentier
pas d'espace pas une aune pas un pied de terre

the emperor/O

london bridge is fall
in down fall

in down

fall
in

down

francaise & pagan
sceptre & orb

crowned by the pope
german & earliest french
man hope

of the christians
destroyer of muslims
defender of rome
aggressor beating against your sins

he was not black enough to be a slaviour
although ill
literate and lack
ing in table manners
he saved eu/rope from the so/called sterile fate of mulattoes

at roncesvalles at roncesvalles at roncesvalles

roland est mort god has taken his armour to heaven
roland est mort god has taken his armour to heaven

pas de piste pas de sentier
pas d'espace pas une aune pas un pied de terre

rome could never be built in a day
could never be here on the rhine

no matter how i wish/no matter how i will/it
so

the pope sleeps on the rock of his feathers
he possesses the secrets of gold and frankincense and ash

bearing the shroud of christ's life of ihs audacious embarkation
he dreams of what he calls one word one world one balm one

unam sanctam

but soon there will be
two

of us

chapel & palace warrior & monastery soulace & sword vegas &
holy father

and rome will be destroyed
at roncesvalles at roncesvalles at roncesvalles

some say it was destroyed when caesar fell
o what a falling off was there my countrymen

when
joshua fit the battle of jericho

when
constantine pressed impressive lips on the petit-christs of the

catacombs

2

but i deny these histories

london bridge is fall
en down fall

en down fall
en down fall

en down

though there could still be harbour here

3

so i imported monks and scholars
paid them well created court encouraged trade

and made myself the master of the armed brigades

with christendom imperialled
it was i self against the saracen

4

and then there was that christmas morning coronation
the ex-barbadian barbarian
crowned by the yoke of rome

the pagan nightingales were singing near the convent of the well
lit sacred
heart

and yes i did not listen

the runic stones retold the stories of my ancestors
but i declined against them   .   *i will build cathedrals*
now that i am king

aachen cologne notre-dame de cap-henri

monasteries of blind imperilled slaves
schools for the outside children of the dead
heed not these ignorant saxonian guerrillas

the nodalbingians the widukind

my constables will crush them
and my clericals will carry the alphabet to the head

waters of the elbe

my cross of boniface
will forever flower along the walls of heresburg

my indian elephants
will trumpet trumpet trumpet trumpet out across the rhine

ah yes my brother christophe

you must force a man to the font and have him make faith
and pay for it in taxes and in tithes and in the tolls of bells

we do not wish to find niggers niggers everywhere
not in aquitaine and certainly not in gaul

these russian slavs must be halted
odin and siegfried and the music of bartok cut

out from their folks & shut
up in the rain

i do not wish to hear of ships
sailing to senegal

of traders stopping off at takoradi
of hawkins naipaul of the middle passage

i do not wish to sit down to tea
with lord constantine

or with miss ping/pong goolagong/i
ching. ken with the junk/ie chine/ee

ch'eng h'siang/is bard enough to bear

5
*london bridge is fall
en down*

*fall
en down*

*fall
en down*

*london bridge is fall
en down*

ban

ban

caliban

Musa

But alcuin has lost
his dear nightingale
modulamine

musae

its body so mound
and dim
have you seen

him the druids
must have injured
him away

how he had hated
the hymns
of the cloister

would you believe
it? rui rui brown
wing señor

tossed
on the blood
heap

he

could not sing
in the dead
heat

Aachen

Now dying at aachen
i prophesy the downfall of the empire
virgil and the pauline virtues

the dialect of the tribes will come beating up against the crack
foundation stones of latin like the salt whip speechless lips
of water eating the soft tones of venice

sparing us back to purest parthenon
to simple anglo saxon chronicle
to ga to gar to derek walcotts pitcher of clear metaphor

masons will then rape this virgin
of her drapery of satin
until she is satan again

botticelli will have wet dreams
about her
even unto the corruption of her navel

da vinci will make her wink
and the portuguese will put her face up for sale
around the markets of the unknown world

i hear of marinus of tyre
of slave ships setting out for sidon
of sycorax the black witch of a small hotel

mercantilism
not the black magnificenti
dei medici will appear in the papers tomorrow

pilots pilates pirates

roland est mort

at roncesvalles at roncesvalles at roncesvalles

and scales of justice tilt towards the west towards the
sun towards the setting islands

Mont Blanc

Rome burns
and our slavery begins

in the alps
oven of europe

glacier of god
chads opposite

industry was envisioned here in the indomitable glitter
it out proportions the parthenon

the colosseum is not to be compared with it
nor dome nor london bridge bernini bronze nor donatello marble

there is more wealth here than with the bankers of amsterdam
more power than in any boulder dam of heaven

volt crackle and electricity it has invented
buchenwald nagasaki and napalm

it is the frozen first atomic bomb
its factories blaze forth bergs and avalanches

its unships sail down rhine down rhone down po down dan down
tiber

to the black sea dead to the world to the red sea of isaias

without it the sahara would have been water
latvium carthage tunis would have been dolphin towns

genoa would have become a finchal of the esquimaux
columbus would have sailed south along the congo's rivers

but being immobil:e here
more permanent than pope or charlemagne

it has burnt rome
but preserved europe

as it rises

chad sinks

sa
hara wakes out slowly

the dry snake of the harm
attan the harmattan reaches into our wells into our smiles in

to our cook
ing pot oil in

to the water re
flecting our walls in

to the bone
of the mutton in

to our dry
gully eyes

and the green brown dunn of sudan of bel uur of the niger
sa

hell

crumbles into these flickering miles miles silences of holes
of noon in our belly

marrow burning its protein to gravel
skin mouldered to ash

holocaust of dome
heads propped up on sticks of skeletones

ball headed children
naked of all else but large deep agate space age eyes

black bladders of dried milk hung haggard from my mannequin
flies dying into crevices of mouths from all the fertile places

with only memories of nipple suck suck suck
ing their blistered lips the flim crew cameras already closing in

like buzz like buzzards on this moonscape manscape in slow
motion

herdsmen becoming scarecrows
their howls of silent dust wheeling across the super

sands like paper
water in the shadow of this snow and ici/cle

this eye
less rise

ing gas
face mountain

Nuum

I

And out of the ground
these men with black faces

they frighten me
they tell of coal

of gaols underground
where they follow the phantoms of vulcan

they have discovered an ancient city of forests
older than the dinosaur or the ice age

they chip it out into black blocks of lamplight
and it warms them with a sun more distant than orion's war

it's this that breathes out of their faces
star winds wrinkles of inner darkness

but it is not equiano it is not paul
robeson it is not othello the moor

they live beyond the mountain in green pastures
where they have not yet bitten the neutron

they still worship gods that make them smile
that allow them to welcome the stranger
that will render them heavily prisoner

2

but these are the miners of the empire

they burn
they eat the land

they vomit it up
they leave lakes of desolation

ochre choler water

that returns no benediction
plantations of dead plankton

ceaselessly
ceaselessly
ceaselessly

clocks ticking to mesh

they destroy
they destroy
they destroy

they do not care

they have cruelled their faces of fire
of fear of the plague. of the ark. of the aaardvark
fresh from the bellows they smile seeds of colonies

they sow islands
basalt and dischord coral among the butterflies
ashanty towns arise and rust within their oxides

confound against their ikons
ash. twits. sparrows
loin cloths with too much old age spaces in them

wild little ones. bewild. ered elders

sarawak
arawak
samarkand

bronze catafalques of benin city

there is hiss.
teria from apertures of foundries
drying fiords gold plated cardiacs

panting triumphant locomotive izukkis
mad explosions of gas of carbide of bhopal blitzkreigs
of mein kampf mein feuhrrherrherr. satellites like discoteques

departing upwards through their own whirling light

and all this benignly
and all this beneficently
the bells of st bernard burn

ing towards them from this whisp/ering scarface mountain

Dies irie

Day of sulphur dreadful day
when the world shall pass away
so the priests and shamans say

what gaunt shadows shall affront me
my lai sharpeville wounded knee
ho chi marti makandal

to what judgement meekly led
my lai harlem wounded knee
fedon fatah sun yat sen

life and death shall here be voice
less rising from their moist
interment hoist

ing all their flags before them
shall men gather trumpeted
by nyabingeh from the dead

day of sulphur guernica
when the world shall pass away
so the priests and pundits che

what gaunt shadows shall appal me
my lai sharpeville wounded knee
to what judgement meekly led

shall men gather trumpeted
by nyabingeh from the dead
life and death shall here be choice

less poniard poison rocket bomb
nations of the earth shall come
nanny mahdi accompong

37

and their record page on page
long march bandung brimestone hill
rodney robeson ras makonnen

burning burning from tomorrow
fears of phantoms that confront
them sentences of righteous rage

if the pious then shall shake me
haile mary full of grace
how will sandinista greet me

what moncadas will he shaka
sentences of righteous rage
haile mary full of grace

if vaqueros then shall bomb
bard babu baboon master racist
what reply will malans make me

what defences will they fascist
verwoerd vvoster pik van botha
which sowetos will they rape

mighty and majestic god
head herder of the lost herero
zulu sioux seminole

what reply will merchants make me
with what phantoms will they bait me
what confessions will they fake

day of sulphur soufriere day
light when no clouds shall pass away
so the priests and showmen say

day of judgement day of sorrow
day for which all sufferers pray
when the sword shall pass away

day of thunder day of hunger
bring me solace bring me fire
give me penance bring me power
grant me vengeance with thy word

X/plosive video tape salesman

Hello
hello
hello
hello

i
am the no

bel peace plize winner
have just invented plunder

the sky of life is in tatters
from the confusion

scattered lanterns weep & peer
about the courtyard of the stars

& there are limits everywhere

brick mortar woodwork
they are all mortal to me now

i
can breach your banks

i
can corrupt your citadels

i
am in easy reachings of your
heart your harbours & your clanks

i
can easily enter you through/this likkle ewer of bleeps

hello
hello
hello
hello

can you hear me?

yes?

i
was trying to say what my name

yes?

i
was trying to

what?

no noise?

did you say
nose?

my eyes drip gun
from the gum

tree & it is dark dark
night in my hedge

hog/what? what

about mouth?

you can't understand what i
shaying?

mumble me then my consonants are locomotives
let me un/couth from end to end of the continent in a syllable of

drumes

what's crack?

it's kkkennedy
the logic of his skull split open in dallas

a red
egg running down the spilt walls of the desert

soon it will be bauxite again
those cedar trees dry rusting in a valley of

laburnium

then the white villages
hidden behind their dreams

& the weight of the rivers
& the blue

mountain slopes
& the hymns

of the nation
& the confeder

ations

& on
& on

& on
& on

until it will be the
president himself of our bandana banana re

public

what did you say your name
was?

sir
addoo whoo?

major general
at whose funeral?

a black hearted card
inal?

i'll offer them peace
or a plize

or a piece
of my plize

or a package

or i'll prize
them open like one

a them condense milk cans
that we shell

instead of real cows & red
rancid sorrow

lower the reefs & let
love come in

open the whores
of the city

my horses my wood/en
troy horses are ready to wage sin

against them

tell your priests to foretell
that a white god falls down from heaven tomorrow

let your scholars write it as history
looks

so that your extra school children can
read all about it read all about it

senior common rooms quibble
about it with cheese biscuit nibble

& wine

make
your national airline get me down there on time

hello
hello
hello
hello

can you see me

now?

yes?

that's me
at the well
llinging the bell

that's me
winding the clock
on the remmington rifle

that's me
slipping the bolt back for the west
at amoy

& clambering down
the trap
doors of troy

that's me
mopping up the mess
at thermopylae

that's me
with the king

that's me
with the cong

that's me
with king kong

i
am locking him

up
in the mekong delta with

blondie

that's me
at the helm with the poison pen & rice

paper/what?

that's me
in the sha

that's me
in the shad

that's me
in the shadow

the valley
the slough
of your pond

that's me
at the forge
sledgehammer of cloud

bellows of hiroshima

that's me
walking away
in the shroud of the flame

what?

what?

what?

what?

no crutch?

there's a space in your head where your eyes

were/what?

cat
cut your

crouch?

da gama gone home with your
luggage?

somebody rapping your
language?

there's that doom in my ear
drums

again

quack?

i can't hear your crack/le

quot?

kwoo?

christ/opher who?

hell/o
hell/o
hell/o
hell/

The visibility trigger

And so they came up over the reefs

up the creeks and rivers
oar prong put put
hack tramp silence

and i was dreaming near morning

i offered you a kola nut
your fingers huge and smooth and red
and you took it your dress makola blue

and you broke it into gunfire

the metal was hot and jagged
it was as if the master of bronze

had poured anger into his cauldron

and let it spit spit sputter
and it was black spark green in my face

it was as if a maggot
had slapped me in the belly
and i had gone soft like the kneed of my wife's bread

i could hear salt leaking out of the black hole of kaneshie
i could hear grass growing around the edges of the green lake
i could hear stalactites ringing in my cave of vision

bats batting my eyes shut
their own eyes howling like owls in the dead dark

and they marched into the village
and our five unready virginal elders met them

bowl calabash oil carafe of fire silence

and unprepared and venerable i was dreaming mighty wind in trees
our circles talismans round hut round village cooking pots

the world was round and we the spices in it
time wheeled around our memories like stars

yam cassava groundnut sweetpea bush
and then it was yams again

birth child hunter warrior
and the breath

which is no more

which is birth which is child which is hunter which is warrior
which is breath

that is no more

and they brought sticks rods roads bullets straight objects

birth was not breath
but gaping wound

hunter was not animal
but market sale

warrior was child

that is no more

and i beheld the cotton tree
guardian of graves rise upward from its monument of grass crying
aloud in its vertical hull calling
for crashes of branches vibrations of leaves

there was a lull of silver

and then the great grandfather gnashing upwards from its teeth
of roots.   split down its central thunder
the stripped violated wood crying aloud its murder. the leaves
frontier signals alive with lamentations

and our great odoum
triggered at last by the ancestors into your visibility
crashed

into history

Alph

Hannibal heavily crossing the alphs
    clangour of armour clamour of ice
    ravings of rock steeples of blue metal

    plunder

Hannibal heavily crossing the alphs
    enamoured with honour
    risking his vigour on the slippery slopes of an elephants

    thunder

    which sibyl slipped him that glacier
    how from his yard did he dream of this mountainous conquest
    how high were the hills that he saw from the poor of his

    house

    was his father born lame bit by machines crushed by a god
    would the hand claps of vodoun have roused
    him could his drums dream these empires

    ump

Hannibal heavily crossing the alphs
    was his father the son/rise of green quetzalcoatl setting out
    in his mental canoe

III

Cap

From the pic of le cap where the citadel sits
the arawaks wait
the fleches of their headdress are bells up the montagne

the rings of the palm trees are bells up the montagne
toussaint is a zemi
he stares from the flesh of the stone

the white of the helmet columbus conquistador
the white of the sword
becomes lightning

the steel of the machete
the knife of the god
thongs of the whips

drink water like trees
africaines from the slave ships
dance out of the riflemen's loins

become dessalines dessalines
la crete-a-pierrot
the spangle of death from the hot

of the trees
and christophe columbus climbs up to his mountain top
with the face of his horse in the faith of his shadow

he stumbles on priest on an ivory slave on a spaniard
the places of pain become pig
snouts the black becomes white becomes black becomes rain

falling to plunder the roof
of the world
toussaint is a zemi

he stares from the stone from the eye
lids of flame
at his fate

And now a soft commentaries from
Angelo Solimann Africanus
the Neumann

1

The new man is nubile
and has made his choice
as priest or politician

police or poet
choirboy or cocks
man

da vinci was the last of the genies
and he knew

it

though we didn't seem to believe in it
then

now the world belongs to machiavell and philip
the second of spain

and to that calculating calvin

is them that working all night long in the high
light executive suites

on all the national security commissions
on all the full plenary sessions

is them who is right what is rote in the paper
is them the master gunners in the sweating three piece suits

who circumcizing caliban

2

the continent leaks outwards from its frontiers
and there is nothing to keep it in its place since charlemagnias
body lies a-mouldring in the grave

gunpowder has destroyed the castle
knights templar of the holy grail ride east
seeking the sources of their power

coeur de lion is becoming aladdin
time to look to your lamplight me friend
lock up the great wail of china

marco is chipping away in his kashmiri polo neck sweater
save me democritus
if it was you who practised those speeches with pebbles in your

mouthings

village me no hounfour
prayer me no virtue no more

say pure
and it comes out poor

say holy
before it comes out dirty shocks

for the church
for the state for the state machine
for the merchant banker

for mm for gigi for mata hari for caesarina borgia
for the sake of the journey
for the slake of this thirst of dunes

will i go now
welcoming the stranger
will i destroy

welcoming the scavenger
will i establish rule
straight tracks cut clattering across the land

eating your head of grapes set greeding on its plate, sir john
i'll roll these barbers back along the carpet of the prairies
until their blacks wail blue against the pisstine u

rals

i'll sink the whole lake of the aztecs on a sunny sundae after
noon

i'll take one i'll take two i'll take free i'll take five
i'll take twenty & two & twenty two hundred & twenty two too

& flake them alive

 two hundred & twenty two thousand two million & two bleaching sea
shells of skulls of too million scallops of closed eyes of lost

eye
lids scattered along the beaches of the belgian congo

i'll build white blazing pyramids of these like chiops
was mine uncle the beaks of doves that coo & curoo in these cotes

pinging their pure enamel

<pre>
                    5
                  o5o
                oo5oo
              ooo5ooo
            oooo5oooo
          ooooo5ooooo
        oooooo5oooooo
      ooooooo5ooooooo
    oooooooo5oooooooo
  ooooooooo5ooooooooo
  oooooooooo5oooooooooo
 ooooooooooo5ooooooooooo
oooooooooooo5oooooooooooo
ooooooooooooo5ooooooooooooo
+oooooooooooo5oooooooooooo+
</pre>

and it could go on for ever & ever & ever

57

soon i will be asked to ask them to forget forgive
their savage homelands their dark & dung & kraal & bantustans

and
call me   bucky massa   yes   yes good   yes god   yes gold

therefore no mud hut villages wearing those pygmy straw
hats you will see within the pages of the phantomb

no afro hair dos in our schools no dialect around the holy house
and on these

premises

AFRICAANSE ONLY EVEN IF YOU NEVER PLEASE

in fact. in order to avoid drop-face and rising cost of expec
tations

there will be no more promises before election time
in fact. there will no longer be election time

and to prevent your people from continuing to break the law
justinian and judisex

we will decode the codex so that to say it soft
(m16s in a sling)

there will be no more legislation
but ruling for the summum bonum with benign deregulation

what pilate call the truth involve this state machine in an x
penditure. a cash flaw problem you might call it that it's

pretty clear no. body can afford

so we'll go back to owls & cyclops eyes & hire us a firm of x/
perts of consulting oracles

who will advise us why wherefore exploit us to our three
bags full. the local raw material of lies

4

without a future
all houses will be condominiums buses towns
landscraped plantations planned like towns

chapel courthouses main guards & supermarket prisons empty church
yards ring a round with roses of barb wire & there will be nearby
maybe a rural area of cows and other cuds

grass
cutters certain prescribed crops & posies proscribed ridges

pasture land

beyond that there is rab & wilderness & terrorists &
cultural gorillas

caliban

we don't want catch no niggers out here no way neither nor any
rasta man nor hippie

nor any kind a dropout buttapan

there will be
no more sonny rollins

practising his tenor sax among the spires of the brooklyn bridge

no john the baptist
making us believe we has to pay for all his mistakes migraine

massacuriman attraction to his locks by herods daughter

there will be
no more magic lanthorn lilies

no fra angelico annunciations

no herb nor obi bush nor blue nor susumba no canefield doctor in
the back dam

glow

no lla lla llaaa illllalla and malcolm is his profit

Titan

Now they burn west

across the christian ocean humming high above the high drift
of the harmattan

lights blinking on/and off/in touch with stars.   the vulcans
slumbering within their bowels

stealthily stealthily stealthily stealthily

they search they search they search out human rights
scandle and damp.   the mist

upon the window panes where we are making love

they disappear in cloud
and come back glinting in white sunshine high above the coral

reefs.   the palm trees sparrows pigeon doves woodpeckers
quetzalcoatl green green glory adoration to a flower fall

guanahani   coyoacan   vera cruz

inland above the tolmec far north above the thun
der of the orinoco up beyond salmon.   jump

the pine trees cold coyote water tendril all along the heaven
of this world that god made with/out adam from my bones

and night came down upon the causeway with the horses hoofs
cylops.   sparks.   fire of popocatepetl still burning in my engine

tetemextitan

and so we fell upon them on the day of pentecost
more than five.   no fifty thousand perished in that lake
alone along the saltway in the thirteenth year

the cycle of the shears and crossroads.   the parrots
crying all night long

and ever as i turned to face them.   i
came back full of arrows darts and stones
for there was water all around & they could hit.   us with impunity

fly condor

inwards towards the night
search out guatomecs darkened heart from your steel

height

knuckle around your talon fist his chains of golden shrimp
and strip him bleed

pinion his caciques
make them kneel before your newly found immortal and your

pestilence

i will let them worship the head of my horse
as they have worshipped mol and moon and white and yucatan
in the house of the dead landlord

for i have determined
to destroy these mosques i call them.   steps
leading down

to growl and grim and slaughter.   steps
leading down
to mouth and growl and akbal.   these sharp slant down

ward steps

sierras in my blood scream.   metal vision blocked down
dark inside my head.   my vizard helmet crying for the light
this club foot god that haunts me

makes me vomit out destroy   destroy though they were
never chantments like these   heard or told in cadiz
salamanca in the legend   of amadis and there were
palaces of stone and cedar   walls painted as if in

egypt

after the fashion   of their calmecac
bird beast bowl   hands
as if always hungry   feathers
of great colourful   confusion

awnings

of cotton cloth and awesome   spattered hieroglyphics of

the underworld
and there was fruit and native   roses and great cisterns of
sweet   water

and birds of many breeds and colours that came into the lake and
gold
enough to

build la scala and the eiffel   tour i swear i had not
seen or heard   or even
dreamed of lands more beautiful than these not in the whole of

africa

i stood there looking out as if i had discovered the pacific
though there was yet no thought of andes inca atahuallpa darien

and so i overturned their idols rolled

them down the stairs and   stare out at you from your
postage   stamps

i

cortez condor clubfoot

evening star

63

Shaman

So dont say i didnt warn you
but you scorned me in mein rags
with my clutch of doves with my leprous nipple

by the waters

there was a nibble of faith
and in the morning i woke up dreaming of surgeons
by the waters

someone was cutting out the colon
of the village there was a djib
of venture in the ghostly clothes

lines soon we would be sailing to by
zantium and satan come
to town i watched the fowlcocks standing to attention

mercedes of the villa dolorosa where is your hearse
and your arrows of san sebastian when i called on you this morn
ing the cards smelled of the gun/man

by the waters

skein of the devil you unravelled knits and spider cob
webs from my whip of screams bell captain of my ship
mates skilled in chains o ebony & ivory o shiloh shennandoa O

black/hole of calcutta

he knew how to dig cane
holes row on row like blue cornish galley slaves wet
sweating buttocks thigh against thormidor inches together

sowing sorrow for the nineteenth century where i sit down and weep

i was to be his caddy on the golf course
the harddough bread of the plantation
green when it was raining

golden brown when ready for the fire
i tossed him up the googeely he taught me
war & speace faith hope & scar/city brother & brotherhood

lums

but his bible blackened them out
and i could not see the light between his pad and the pavilion
what shall we do with gary sobers and pythagoras

those gentle pythons and investigators o jerusalem

shots/where before leaves satisfied
the fm radio/where before we lived in the clean ear of our wisdom
plastic/where before there were cool claypots in the land O

babylon

when i saw where rome was burning
i cried out jesus christ was the hanged man of industrial

birmingham

but you called me alabama pigeon
fink and stoned me into silence on my stony

hill

i cried out that these sticks you brought into the village were
x
plosives and not olive

branches

but you had me heckled into liver
spots and now i cannot be auditioned for the coalgate tv talent

66

show

i warned you that miss universe was not the only virgin mary
but you played me fauré's requiem in agnus dei stereo
using a monographic stylus on the grooved papyrus dark

i had wanted to rap it all out

how dangerous were the generosities wrapped up in cellophane
& xmas paper you'd paddle up onto the beaches of cipango and up
into the darkened reaches of the man/grove swamp

but you rang me out of the village which is now wired for sound
sound systems space eye dishes disco brams eel
ectronic micro/maniacs & wayside preachers harps

i just can't get/up stand/up stand/up for i rights bob
marley in this ya ghetto too much live i now in this wild evil
world of axles wrecked gear boxes scatter/pillar levers

the huge red silent pain of dead. fish dead. car screams
their lobster sponges dried out breathe
ing rasp & rust and rasspan angles banggalang & booming babylon

&

life/line biscuit bins
so. prano tins
tom. toms of bathtub tombs abandoned by the marat sade

i still dream dreams harbour hallucinations tune in to cable
metro/color visions
and feed them to myself

hello

and cannot share with you my cornmeal porridge in the wet &
morn
ing glow

i see the towers rising russian red beyond the dungle
and i have heard the names of the strange architects you plaster
paris on them crying each to each

by the waters by the waters where i sit down to reap

Mai Village

You see it rusting there
sauteurs maggotty six mens bay
small delightfully unspoiled
the guide books say

on a fair
day you can see the ancestors grey
headed guardians who toiled
like gully slaves to give their homes away

there was a fear
for a time that marcus malcolm martin & mahatma one of the sooth
say/ers from among the youth might have boiled
over boys will be boils they say

but they chew gum sitting on the wall in sunshine or in a sha. a. dow
steer clear of politricks letting the future pray
unto itself with garbage & kwashiorkor freakouts of tropical vio
lets sore foot shak shak & nigger blooming sirius

& jean rhys hummingbirds of coulibri decay

Donna

Is escape dem-a farr
musk rose blooms

the tight room with its oils drying clothes
stale mask of nivea scream

the skin drying of wet
the mattrass dying of sweat

she will not open the window for fear of intruders
yesterday the girl raped in the toilet of the carib cinema
by four fourteen year ol' yout'

yesterday the girl raped coming home from school
yesterday the girl raped in her own house in her own home in her
own bed and all her dolours taken

the room stifles the forehead as the necchi sings
if she had had a child it would have been a girl/sleeping
or a boy sucking his thumb pushing his soles through the hole in
the blanket

yu want out de light?

the breasts small and familiar
coconut oil as she stands close

the rayon slip on thin as skin now
luminous with flesh

black span of dark
ness your bridge to her world

texcoco tenochtitlan

and she arch
ing glowing closer

curving as the world curves as the evening curves
the wind like a soft fresh of flowers her almond of silence

she enters your soul
displacing your anger the days useless lumber
and lets it explore you

converting you prone to columbus
some eyeless african sailor
and brings you home hero

encircled with flowers confetti of love blinding you
but she is locked still in her island
your key will click responsive to its prick

of heat the gear will shift its metal tendons snort
ing wheels tearing the gravel as darkness explodes
in the engine the owls of headlights blinking on at the gateway

an lard how it hot how a greasy
and de pickney dress dem fe done

an de lang track a night tick tickin tick tickin
machine petal shattering on
an de clock stuck at 1.35 1.35 1.35 1.35

see how me yeye cyaan prop open even
an de rent fe pay
an anoder one comin tomarrow

an who will memember dem ancient a days dat a walkin to school
walkers wood ocho rios
how a prangalang down to camperdown town

an de man want i sleep wid im
an me got me exam

an de man seh mek i go wid im
an me can barely bear to look pan im

but wha yu guh do when yu belly gone slack an yu young gifted
an na idiot . . .

im drive away now
me glad glad

iator

in im company char
in im chariat

while i sittin down here wid dis fine toot comb
tryin to scratch out de lies dat a tell

cause a girl got to learn not to get too ole
not to let it look dat she belly gone cole

for dese man who is here tonight an tomarrow dem gaane . . .

Nam

Out of this roar of innumerable demons

hot cinema tarzan sweat
rolling moth ball eyes yellow teeth
cries of claws slashes clanks

a faint high pallor

dust

oceans rolling over the dry sand of the savanna

your houses homes warm still with the buffalos milk
bladder of elephant tusk of his stripped tree
sing soft clinks

but the barracks

the dark dark barks of the shark
boys
the cool juice of soweto . . .

out of this dust they are coming
our eyes listen out of rhinoceros thunder
darkness of lion

the whale roar stomping in heaven
that black bellied night of hell and helleluia
when all the lights of anger flicker flicker flicker

and we know somewhere there there is real fire
basuto mokhethi namibia azania shaka the zulu kenyatta the shatt
erer the maasai wandering into the everlasting shadow of jah

daughters lost daughters

bellowing against bullhorn and kleghorn
bellowing against bargwart and the searchlights of dogs
bellowing against crick and the kick in the stomach

the acrid wretch against the teeth
bellowing against malan malan malam malan
and boer and boerwreck and boertrek and truckloads of metal

helmet and fusil and the hand grenade
and acid rhodes and the diamonds of oppenheimer
the opulence of voortresshers the grass streiders . . .

suddenly like that fire that crows in johannesburg
you were there
torn. in tears. tatters

but the eyes glittered and the fist
clenching around that scream of your mother bled
into a black head of hammers

and the light fell howl
on soweto

the night fell howl
on soweto

and we who had failed to listen all. those. foot. steps
who had given you up like a torn paper package

your heroes   burning in your houses
               rising from your dust bowls
               flaring from the sky

               listen now as the news items lengthen
               gathering like hawks looking upward like the
               leopard plunging into the turmoil like the

               constrictor

and that crouch/shot
shout out against that beast and pistol
the police who shot patrice who castrated kimathi

and clattering clattering clattering clattering
the veldt's gun metal's wings
rise from their last supper their hunger of bones

bomba

and the daniels sing

>   *ukufa akuqheleki kodwa ke*
>   *kuthiwa akuhlanga lungehlanga*
>   *lalani ngenxeba nikhuzeka*

>   and we are rowing out to sea where the woman
>   lived with her pipe and her smoke
>   shack

>   and her tea in the tea
>   pot
>   tankard of hopes

>   herbs

>   *lamagora afele*
>   *izwe lawo*

>   and we are rowing out to sea
>   where there were farms

>   and our farmers laid waste the land
>   to make honey. we are the bells of the land . . .

dumminit
dumminit

lit by lantern and lamp
damp

dumminit

ash/can
kero

sene glow
can

dle &
glare

dumminit

hitting the head of the hanvil

huh

drumminit

his schoolbook
huh
but to learn
blood
what is blood
huh
to bless
dream
and that hill now under the ocean
and the pages splashed with his blood
and that bullet a hero hero herero . . .

once the germans destroyed every sperm
in your village every man who could walk
every nim growing into the noom and nam of his man/hood

they stripped skin and made catapults skulls were their pelmets
upon the wall
and the torn feet cracked and stacked and streggaed

rubbish heap. dog howl. cenotaph

and for days there was stench over the grasslands
and for months there was silence upon the trees
cow . goat . udder . manyatta

bantustan upon the land . . .

and then it was gone like all hero hero herero
like your canoe upon the land . . .

walking back down now from the shores of kikuyu water
washing back down now from swahili laughter

zimbabwe kinshasa limpopo
always limpopo the limper the healer

it comes down from the ruins of the north
from the lakes of the luo

from the sunlights and sunrise of the east

as ancient as sheba as wise as the pharaohs
as holy as the early morning mists of ityopia

an i
man
tek long
time to
reach hey
but a
bomb
an de lim
popo drop
down
an de
dread
come
an de
wreck
age soon
done

soon

soon

soweto

we have waited so long for this signal
this howl of your silence
this heat of herero this hero

and i beheld the great beast strangled howling in its own chains
led by the fetlocks
and the opulence useless
and the guns shattered and silent

bongo man a come
bongo man a come

bruggadung
bruggadung

bruggadung
bruggadung

78

.

and we rise

mushroom

mau

kilimanjaro

silvers of eagles

tears

savannas

nzingas of rivers

umklaklabulus of mountains

and the unutterable metal of the volcano

.

rising

rising

rising

burning

soon

soon

soon

soweto

bongo nam a come
bongo nam a come

X/Self's Xth Letters from the Thirteen Provinces

I

Dear mamma

i writin you dis letter/wha?
guess what! pun a computer o/kay?
like i jine de mercantilists!

well not quite!

i mean de same way dem tief/in gun
power from sheena & taken we blues &

gone . . .

say
what?/get on wi de same ole

story?

okay
okay

okay
okay

if yu cyaan beat prospero
whistle?

.
no mamma!

is not one a dem pensive tings like ibm nor bang & ovid
nor anyting glori.   ous like dat!

but is one a de bess tings since cicero o
kay?

.
it have key
board &

evva

ting. like dat ole
remmington yu have pun top de war. drobe up there ketchin duss

only dis one yu na ave to benn down over & out
off de mistake dem wid white liquid paper. de papyrus

ribbid & soff

before it drei up flakey &
crink. like yu was paintin yu house

um doan even nuse no paper yu does have to roll
pun dat black rollin pin like yu rollin dough pun a flatten

& does go off ping pun de right hann wing a de paper
when de clatterin words start to fly & fling like a ping. wing

.
wid dis ting so now
long before yu cud say jackie robb
inson r. t-d2 or shout

quink

dis obeah blox
get a whole whole para
graph write up &

quick
pun a black
bird like

dat indonesia fella in star
trick
where dem is wear dem permanent crease up grey

flannel cost
umes like dem gettin ready to
jogg

but dem sittin down dere in such silence a rome
it not turn
in a hair pun dem wig/wam &

hack/in out hack/in out hack/in out all sorta read
out & fall
out & garbage & ting from all part/icles a de gal. axy

mamma

a doan know how pascal & co/
balt & apple & cogito ergo sum
come to hinvent all these tings since

de rice & fall a de roman empire
& how capitalism & slaveley like it putt christianity
on ice

so dem cud always open dat cole
smokin door a hell when dem ready for a psalm sangridge or
choke

.
why i cyaan nuse me hann & crawl up de white like i use
to?

since when i kin
type?

dats what i tryin to tell
ya!

yu know me cyaan
niether flat
foot pun de key

boards like
say charlie
chap dance/in

far

less touch
tapp/in like
bo/

jangles

walk/in
down chauncery

lane/yu
hearin me
mwa?

but i
mwangles!

a mean
a nat farwardin wid star
wars

nor sing
songing bionic
songs or like sputnik &

chips

goin bleep bleep bleep bleep bleep bleep bleep into de peloponnesian
wars

but i
mwangles . . .

2

Why a callin it
x?

a doan writely
know

but yesterday when a was tellin a ceratin girl
frenn about

it she kinda look at i funny like if
she think i has xerxes

or aids

so she soffly soffly silk/
in i off like if i down sick/

ly or sorrow or
souse

but is like what i tryin to sen/seh &
seh about muse/

in computer &
learnin prospero linguage &

ting

not fe dem/not fe dem
de way caliban

done

but fe we
fe a-we

for not one a we should responsible if prospero get curse
wid im own

curser

though um not like when covetous ride miss praedial
mule

but is like we still start
where we start/in out start/in out start/in out start/in

out since menelek was a bwoy & why
is dat & what is de bess weh to seh so/so it doan sounn like

brigg
flatts nor hervokitz

nor de pisan cantos nor de souf sea
bible

nor like ink. le & yarico & de anglo saxon
chronicles

&

a fine
a cyaan get nutten

write

a cyaan get nutten really
rite
while a stannin up here in me years & like i inside a me shadow

like de man still mekkin i walk up de slope dat e slide
in black down de whole long curve a de arch

i

pell

ago

long

long

ago

like a

tread

like a

tread

like a

tread

mill

or mile

stone

or pet

like a pet

like a perpet.

ual plant

or

plantation &

mamm/ a

a know yu can plant lettice or nice but yu cyaaan eat
ikebana

.
yet a sittin down here in front a dis stone
face/eeee

lectrical mallet into me
fist

chipp/in dis poem onta dis tablet
chiss/ellin darkness writin in light

like i is a some/ is a some/ is a some
body/ a

x
pert or some

thing like moses or aaron or one a dem dyaaam isra
lite

&
mam

why is
dat?

what it
mean?

Twoom

In that whole room
   schoolchildren callin c/a/t cat mouse
                       r/a/t rat house

   under the trees
   murder the sun/rain/wind/blizzard of dust

   under the trees
   a child squats in its own blood. mid

   wife of severance

in that whole room
   trolleys masks drip/salt/drip/salt/needle
   the baby mothers bawlin for deliverance

in that one room
   where you could harbour hundreds from the dread & doubt
   the ninety ninety year old women rescued from mid
   night rust

in that whole room
   which could have harboured bell & belly
   woman fever ward & always someone elses mothers blast
   ed neglect bones cast into ebb tide homes

in that whole room
   them have this one white disem/boy
   this one white disembody mannequin
   art/istically ex/ploded on a white mat on the pavé floor

   surrounded by like 23 white plaster for
   nicalia cats some bigger than the
   smaller ones but all the same way all

the same way looking all the same way
in the same
direction silent sitting on white silent boxes

in that one room
in that fantastik room

and in one corner
all alone
really all all alone &

white

still white still
life
one little one

still kit
still plaster
plastic cat

a likkle bo
peep
black sheep

cat

while on the street
outside

while on the corner of our life
outside

while on the edge & corner of our natal knife
outside

a   black man sweeping sweeping paper waste

nine miles of black star liners gut and gutters strife
dead dogs dead cats dead fowlcocks strangled in their crows

dead crows dead cast off cruelties

plastic and plaster and dead tubes squeezed dry
of all their open locks to strong & clean & beauty

of all their how they laughed his children centuries ago
before this present hunger on the pavement here

lifts carefully against the wind a matches to his kerosene
and angry paper face

and i know now
the mother of five pickney i will drop to red gal ring to/morrow
night

to/night
will have no other love to offer those live lips
but borrow me a porridge ya

and this one leaf a ceresee drop in a pan a water

and vultures raking over kingston and the dead race courses
smoking at caymanas near the cooking stones

the peoples liberation army surrendering to sodom & gomorrah
in their bvds

to no mcarthur on the deck of aircraftcarrier nimitz of no name

in that whole room
in that whole air-conditioned room

sipping its own silence in the well
lit gloom

who kill
the cat

who bell
the mannequin

IV

Stone

High up in this littered world of rock. stone

yucca bush bamboo trash narrow
defiles where there are no sweet painted trees

wind we know always sharp slant sleet howl but warm
as your lips and gentle as a mother with her baby cheek
to cheek misty mornings high noons spectacular sunsets

at the bottom of this high world high above it all we draw
the lion. picket our stand and make our testament
boy girl woman warrior elder statesman gunsmith technician food
engineer shamir shama shaman we are all gathered here

guerrilla camouflage flack. jacket
ambuscade thorny stockade. we smell
our cooking and our evening
smoke. the little ones collect
the firewood. i feel

the fire flickering my back. even from five hundred paces
in this hammock
everything looks inwards to this centre
we are not taken lightly in our cups
or in our sleeping bags shocked by surprise
the sentinels along our lifeline ledge of echoes

come down the hill at sunrise with eyes that red the dark
m16s that are not
crutches
though we might hold them o so casual against our sides

we have been visited by goddesses and loan sharks from across the
water. from lome and from abidjan
we make the same blue cloth they make we mix our mortar

similar. our tongues are always rough and bark like theirs
from the same bissi
when children suck their fingers after we have weaned them
from their mother's best breast suppligen
we paint the same green aloes on their slimy biscuits
and wonder if they ever going to learn there's mullet shrimp
and janga in the rivers and ganja in the harvest valley villages
and gungo peas behind the pissitoires

and yet today the hawks on their warm rising roundabouts
look like dark sorrows for the portuguese
have beaten us at last at their own game
surrounded us camped hard all year against us. caius
revved rockets up into the very kidneys of our cooking pots
beguiled the younger female fauns with foolish fans and beauty
contestants. have taught them how to shave midden hair and brave
ly bear a buonorott' bikini sheer & mare & tender
loin & how i gonna bring you in an early morning breakfast plate

tourists let inwards by the sweeper at the market gate
rush in and shoot us with their latest nikons and many of our men
are lured away to work at chipping ice in sin
cinnati cutting the canal at christopher
columbus place in panama to scraping braille off battleships
blind grey green waters under
bellies: vieques porto bello choc guantanamo bahia O
black cat nanny nanahemmaa do not desert us now don't let the
harmattan come riding high in here sieve sand through

intestine and wickerwork cassava matapee
prick grit through fish its open golden underwater eye dry
all the all day long sky water up
so that the hillslides come out yellow yellow yellow & catch
fire in the morning grow. so
that the leaves of callaloo will quail. so
that we cannot plant olodumare yam even in this high
tinder season

i remember the dogs here
runagate
runagate
harsp breath bleak teeth the tongue that sees all
runagate
runagate
runagate

i remember the red raider high up on his horse
spur like an eagle thorn
hibiscus spurting from the rearing flanks
drumming upon my head at noon
my blind eye torn out looted
runagate

i remember the chain
and the chain gang sweat
and the gong gong of disaster
runagate
runagate

did i escape the sharp dark crystal graze of the square
foot dog for this
the shooken sugar factory furnace door of the plantation blaze
for this

runagate
runagate
runagate

look how our villages are grown up tall
into this strangled city

tales of another leader lost

solares   bolivare   palanquin

washed away with the frogs and the river and the mud & accompong

runagate
runagate
runagate

Sunsong

And so the drought has dried my tropic
my mellow suns
my fat banana green

termites wings visit me
spindles of tamarind leaves
falling through yellow light

i walk the streets of easter's april
welcomed by crickets
the creak of cicada grass dry as grasshopper husks

tips of the rain
are stardrops that listen listen listen
but do not fall

kaieteur's curved crashing to dryness
sticks crying to dust in the desert
the glistening sand in the distance

our houses are snells

deliver me cold skeletone
branched like bare trees
for journeys lit by stars

my bones sing with dry honey
combs. bees
burrow in cinder and ash

on its black crest of flesh
the harmattan rides
the flowers return to the fire

trumpet cock cat
cattle call triller
they are all alive in the fire

ears of grass grow out of the crackles of paper
rips grope where the petalled heat passes
liquid the roar liquid the yellow clearing

consuming itself the mouth eats air
the dark identifies itself with every gape. and flaring
craze eyed our child grows thin with thirst/y

knowledge. where shall his his
tory permit my cup of penitence to drip
when antelopes of hunger come to breed

his mother fears the knock hears the dread
rock/steady beat of bailiff on her blood and board
lock

out of moonlight. look
out on howl/ers of starved dogs
limp limp

ing cattle. fields burnt to bleak
anger. cinders of sweetness. cracked crystal
the stars tick tick within your pregnant humus

i would leave wood
and dance
i would leave leaf leave blood

leave citadel leave house of bone
i would leave pool
and dance

leave moss and musk and musty corner
stones
i would leave stone. and dance

i would leave dross

i would still say with cesaire. spark
i would say. storm. olodumare's conflagration
i would speak sperm. and twinkle

spirit of the fire
red river of reflection
vermilion dancer out of antelope

i summon you from trees
from ancient memories of forests
from the uncurling ashes of the dead

that we may all be cleansed

Citadel

So
we are learning
we are learning

surrounded by thickets
clustered against my brothers
muskets growing our own thorns

and from each spike and sparkle
each drip of star and lighted water candle
the petals of dead planets broken

cusps from which i have now stumbled
links fragments obscure breastplates
still hearting us together

o sisyphus o herculean labourer

unto the humble herb and straggeling idiot of the tribe
the vultures flying over christophe's citadel
itself still sailing where the islands float

unmoored and moisture lidded laden with dream and dew
and find no anchor of love here no hope in our back
yard we find no safe no hollow

but here in the cup of my word
on the lip of my eyelid of light
like a star in its syllable socket

there is a cripple crack and hobble
whorl
of colour   eye
at last   cool harbour

death of the trapped fish is not its meaning
dearth of the quetzalcoatl wing is not within its memory
safe for ships the fishermers windjammer

soft cloud   high shadow

ulysses cuts his white teeth towards it
as does my father and the caribs and yemajaa

there is the smell of tar of mango tang
locked sun of oranges and leaking muscovado casks

graph stains of charcoal from the castries mountain
the stretched skin of the brown decks creaking with wave heave

the seas drummers

softly softly on sound fire of spar in the star
light blazed by white bellows the black bulk heaving starboard

it is a beginning

forests canefields move over the waters towards it
seeds of our salt fruit cashew seagrape fatpork macca quickstick

palm

with its blind tendril freedom
a long way the one eyed stare of the coconut will travel

steered by its roots what its milk teaches

till its stalk with its flag and its cross
sword its mailed head and chained feet

walks over the arawaks beaches

2

so write this poem wood
that inches out towards its edges rule the rule
that will need blood the blood

that will devour iron the iron
metal speaking freely of the fire the fire
harp blaze howling hot and long and lambent in the grip of god

so we make pots
potients against the sound of lamentations
against the maljo blowing from the devil's ridge

against thij history that will not write us up unless we lying
down
beneath your raj and spur and raleigh beneath your hiss of drake

across the land
and from this tennament this sipple spider space we hold
we make this narrow thread of silver spin the long time of sand

Ice/Nya

And so the greeks return and are recognized
and so are the ithacans and the battlements of troy

virgil invents aeneas as they set out for civilization
with wounds nourished in the bloodstreams of angst

pyramids come down to the rivers to drink
ankh osiris isis

and you make of me mysteries foundationless histories
child drake athlete moor

when i sleep you say drink
when awake you hear the apes muttered insurrections at the holl
ow door

and all the while kilimanjaro widens deepens darkens wound whole
absence
before your glass before your glacier smoke dreams mist whiteness

unglitter
of sunlight gutter i bleed in now
as

2

rome burns
and our slavery begins

herod herodotus the tablets of moses are broken
the soft spoken

whips are uncoiled on the rhine on the rhone on the tiber
severus the unlocked tiger of wounds lacerate me

syracuse is a white rumble of desolation
the train drifts slowly here slowly
as the last lava of the volcano

look i stretch forth this prayer
and it snaps like a mined thread against me

my hurls collapse without their cornerstones of verbs
i rust at the corneas where there should have been salt
where there should have been a curtain brightness in the brain

3

rome burns
and our slavery begins

sails cannot hold wind
drums cannot remember annunciations

dawn will not be able to hoist festivals
bringing the steel pan bands men over the river in wooden ferries

how will i know that that click of camera camel humped mohammed
will not convert you from island to islam
tourist to perfect terrorist

    i cannot live on olives

    they have been brought by strange smiling brownskinned
    merchants who smell of disaster

    i desire the yams of ibadan
    the lambs of the lake shores of the luo

and yet the yam climbs fist over fist up its green flag
pole and is a discoteque of silver worms

the god eating ijs own flesh of flashing lights
of dribble dust and rock

stone

4

rome burns
and our slavery begins a gutteral of snapping wires

the old man with his carrion bag
uncle macoute

with head of eyes closed
rows of organ teeth smiling smiling

gnashing in combat with the knife
crackelling the neck

lace of my spine and my forgotten kingdom
borne down the padway

on the decrepit riddim of an ass
my gnarled harms clutch/ing clutch/ing

5

        and so your holy mountain digs me down
        its holly whiteness rising
        howls from the depth of lakes
        blackness of gut and gulag

        darkness of ghule and gullet
        rots and fireflies from the dried throats of cisterns
        of silence snarl
        ing knee down to dumbness where no silver will flow

as the vultures wheel back over kingstons over the dead
horses smoking at caymanas over the marble wide umbrella of the

place where rodney freezen in im roman toga
over lord nelson with im one hand

pee
ing out to sea over the shoals and the eels and the glint

ing shields of the sea shells

they wheel high over mona and the mona passage and moncada
and the white marl

of the arawaks and the bay of pigs and the isle of pines
and the fountains of youth and the everglades and the drowned

gardens of atlantis and the slaves graves rocking underwater
hammocks there

fretting their fleuves they steeple upwards into mexico back up
towards

tetemextitlan and popocatepetl
and on towards the thousand red eyes of the andes

illimani arequipa coropuna yerupaja cotopaxi ruiz

6

    & so my trees contract inward
    back into bole into furl into calyx

    black hole of hallelujah
    roots draw themselves into curled shields like shells

    fruit fall
    and their death is devoured by birds that have grown
    ancient scales

    and lakes of glimmer
    rush backwards to their pebbles the pebbles
    of the desert rising to meet me beyond the tramp of mars

V

Xango

Hail

there is new breath here

huh

there is a victory of sparrows

erzulie with green wings

feathers sheen of sperm

hah

there is a west wind
sails open eyes the conch shell sings hallelujahs

i take you love at last my love
my night my dream my horse my gold/en horn my africa

softly of cheek now
sweet of pillow

cry
of thorn

pasture
to my fire

we word with salt this moisture vision
we make from vision

black and bone and riddim

hah

there is a gourd tree here
a boy with knotted snakes and coffle wires

a child
with water courses valleys clotted blood

these tendrils knitted to the cold
un

pearl and wail
the earth on which he steps breaks furl

in rain

bow

tears

the
tiger clue

is his

the bamboo
clumps the bougainvillea

bells

his syllables
taste of wood of cedar lignum vitae phlox

these gutterals
are his own mon general mon frere

his childhood of a stone
is rolled away he rings from rebells of the bone his liberated day

2

over the prairies now
comanche horsemen halt

it is the buff the brown the rose
that brings them closer

the thousand tangled wilful heads
bull yellow tossing

the stretch the itch the musk
the mollusc in the nostril

the flare of drum
feet plundering the night from mud to arizona

the bison plunge into the thunders river
hammering the red trail blazing west to chattanooga

destroying de soto francisco coronado

un
hooking the waggons john

ford and his fearless cow
boy crews j

p morgan is dead
coca cola is drowned

the statue of liberty's never been born
manhattan is an island where cows cruise on flowers

3

and all this while he smiles carved terra cotta
high life/ing in abomey
he has learned to live with rebellions

book and bribe
bomb
blast and the wrecked village

he is earning his place on the corner
phantom jet flight of angels
computer conjur man

he embraces them all

for there is green at the root of his bullet
michelangelo working away at the roof of his murderous rocket

he anointeth the sun with oil
star.tick.star.tick.crick.et.clock.tick

and his blues will inherit the world

4

he comes inward from the desert
with the sheriffs

he flows out of the rivers out of the water
toilets with shrimp and the moon's monthly oysters

he comes up over the hill/slide with grave
diggers he walks he walks

in the street with moonlight with whistles with police kleghorns
with the whores pisstle

5

after so many twists
after so many journeys
after so many changes

bop hard bop soul bop funk
new thing marley soul rock skank
bunk johnson is ridin again

after so many turns
after so many failures pain
the salt the dread the acid

greet

him
he speaks
so softly near

you

hear
him
he teaches

face
and faith
and how to use your seed and soul and lissom

touch
him
he will heal

you

word
and balm
and water

flow

embrace
him
he will shatter outwards to your light and calm and history

your thunder has come home

NOTES

The poetry of *X/Self* is based on a culture that is personal—i-man/Caribbean —and multifarious, with the leaning and education that this implies. Because Caribbean culture has been so cruelly neglected both by the Caribbean itself, and by the rest of the world (except for spot/check and catch-ups via cricket and reggae), my references (my nommos and icons) may appear mysterious, meaningless even, to both Caribbean and non-Caribbean readers. So the notes . . . which I hope are helpful, but which I provide with great reluctance, since the irony is that they may suggest the poetry is so obscure in itself that it has to be lighted up; is so lame, that it has to have a crutch; and (most hurtful of all) that it is bookish, academic, 'history'. Which therefore makes my magical realism, the dub riddims and nation language and calibanisms appear contradictory: *how could these things come from a learned treatise?* The impression, in other words, is that I write the poems from the notes, when in fact I have to dig up these notes from fragments, glimpses, partial memories (it would take a lifetime to track them all down), and the only satisfaction I get is the fascination of watching the counterpoint emerge of 'fact' versus the 'fiction' of the poetry . . . In many cases, like you, am I reading these Notes for the first time . . .

EKB

pages 5–9

severus: African-born Roman emperor and imperial military campaigner. Many of the personae from 'the Ancient World' who appear in this sequence (and in the poem generally) are black, African, slave, brown, creole, Latin, Asian, Alexandrine or Byzantine (or reputedly so; though sometimes, for various reasons, denied of this in some cahiers), for instance:
herod, moses, severus (above), *nikarios, saladin, othello, vercingetorix; che, kismet, ho chi minh, julia, aaron, nancy* (ananse); *naphthali, tutankhammen, aesop, alcmar* (alcman), *socrates, mohammet; ayub khan, shiva, mahatma gandhi, legba l'ouverture, hirohito.*

the tribes . . . vercingetorix . . . arvenin . . . caesar . . . julia: 'Caesar gave *Pompey* his daughter *Julia* in marriage [though in the magical realism of the poem, she also appears later as Caesar's sister, a *'long gowned token television star*'] . . . Next he obtained the province of Gallia Cisalpina, Gallia Transalpina, and Illyrium; and passing into Gaul (58 BC) for nine years conducted those splendid campaigns ['*unlocked tiger of wounds*'] by which he completed the subjugation of the West to Rome. In his first campaign he vanquished the ['*creole*'] Helvetii and Ariovistus; in 57 BC the Belgic confederacy and the *Nervii* . . . He next drove two invading [creole] German *tribes* across the *Rhine* and (55 BC) invaded Britain . . . Visiting northern Italy, he had hastily to return [to Gaul] in midwinter to quell a general rebellion ['*the*

113

tribes the tribes are arising'] headed by young *Vercingetorix* ...' (from *Chambers Biographical Dictionary* (1897/1946) (p.165), given me as Sixth Form Book Prize, Harrison College, Barbados, 1950).

che . . . kismet . . . castro . . . ho chi minh: Third World liberators.

square blue holes in the ruined/colosseum: the colosseum is of course arched. That these have become squares indicates that something is wrong; gone inorganic; which is why '*rotundas topple*'; why '*missiles/prison systems*' are created; why the world is '*flattened*', why '*Chad sinks*' ('Edge of the desert', 'Mont Blanc'), why 'the lake/dead' ('Nix'), why the 'real' becomes 'negatively surreal' in part 3 of 'The papal state machine', with '*would be healers festering like mangoes at the bottom of the bag*' and '*scholars whose minds will smile like cheese/their ragged theses straggeling to please the new demonsthenes*'. See also 'The visibility trigger'.

aaron hammurabi dracon: law-givers.

jordie: the spelling might be wrong, but this refers to the British Northumberland borderlands 'pacified' by Hadrian, Caesar and Severus, projected by the poem also into the modern industrial world, both in Europe ('*o bordeaux o engine driving manchester*') and N. America ('*eternal winter of niagara/falls*').

nancy: Ananse, West African/Caribbean spider/god of tricks, stratagems, transformations, disputations, Nommo/The Word, and of 'fallen' creativity. He ('*sipple spider space*') and his web ('*narrow thread of silver*') appear at the end of 'Citadel'.

harm/attan: dry, drought-causing wind of the Sahara (*sa/hell*, in 'Mont Blanc') pervading the poem.

coarse-grained socrates: one of the best portraits of this philosopher, showing him black, toga'd, rounding, balding (from a fifth-century BC Greek statue in the British Museum) is to be found in a most unexpected quarter: the *Oxford Junior Encyclopaedia*, Vol. 5 (1953/1960), p. 420.

legba: crippled (hence '*limpopo the limper*', in 'Nam') Haitian/Dahomean god of the threshold, of openings (Toussaint *l'ouverture*).

l'ouverture: Toussaint L'Ouverture, slave rebel leader who liberated St Domingue/Haiti from France and the French plantocracy (1791–1804). He was given the sobriquet 'L'Ouverture' in acknowledgement of this; he created an opening for his people. Or, in terms of *vodoun*, the Dahomean culture of the St Domingue slaves, he was *legba* (above), *loa* of thresholds and beginnings. Some portraits of Toussaint picture him, in fact, dwarfed, apparently deformed and unprepossessing, like Legba.

corbusier: Le Corbusier, Swiss-born 1920s architect and habitat philosopher, best known for his monastery at La Tourette, near Lyons, France; the modern community living space, L'Unité, at Marseilles and (in the 1950s) new cities at Chandigarh (Punjab) and other parts of India.

thor . . . gaar . . . baldur: Norse gods.

marrakesh messaoud edjebi atshan . . . fort gouraud lake faguibini: Saharan 'oases of the coconut'.

blue: West Sudanic dye and cosmetic.

Late in the 1960s, as a result of the second Black Renaissance (Black Power, The Black Revolution), the United States gave us our first black (some say 'coloured', 'mulatto') prime time TV show, 'Julia', starring Diahann Carroll in an 'uptown' role. The latest (1985–6) black 'prime time' (not/no longer *'late late'*) US TV show is Bill Cosby's.

apollo: Greek god (of music) and Black Harlem temple (of music).

tina: Tina Turner, well known pop/rock diva of the 1960s and 80s; took part in the record-breaking United States for Africa famine relief video, *'We are the world'*.

montgomery (Alabama) *bus boycott*: start (1956) of Black US Civil Rights Movement led by Dr Martin Luther King, Jr. The Montgomery Bus Boycott was inspired by the action of a quiet back lady, Rosa Parks, who one day decided that she was 'just too plain tired' to move all the way to the black of the racially segregated bus she had boarded.

stars falling on alabama: reference not only to international attraction to Alabama as a result of the Civil Rights Movement, but to popular song, best known perhaps in the Woody Herman jazz version, 'Stars fell on Alabama'; probable reference to super/natural phenomenon.

posse (posse comitatus): a Sheriff's sworn-in volunteer group, got together to run down crooks (especially in 'Westerns'); now being used by W. Atlantic blacks to mean a social/community in group, bound together by a specific (sound) 'system' or disco.

sagres: HQ of Prince Henry the Navigator of Portugal; from this promontory and vantage, he directed the 15th century exploration of the world, especially south along the W. African coast, en route to India and the Far East. The compass (*'chip of metal . . . on a sea of mercury'*) was developed here.

Here is magical montage with a vengeance: Caesar as Richard Nix, crossing the Rubicon in a *'red catallac'*, the rape of the *'sabine drum majorettes'*, *'vinegar instead of coca cola'*, Roman Capitol become St Peter's dome become Washington, DC, become *'ruined/colosseum'* (see 'Salt') *'when the dome/break'*; the *'ides of march'* becomes the *'day* [bay] *of pigs'*, that ill-fated Caesarean 1961 expedition against Revolutionary Cuba, and other imperial defeats: *sauteurs* (French Amerindian Grenada 1654: a last-ditch stand on the fortified heights, like the Jewish Masada, except that the name occurs in no index of standard Caribbean history); Dien Bien Phu (French Indochina/ Vietnam 1954) (*diem biem phu* in the poem).

cong john brown . . . jack/johnson: Third World guerrilla freedom fighters/ rebels ('terrorists'): [viet]*cong. john brown*, the (white) abolitionist who led the raid on Harper's Ferry which signalled the start of the American Civil War (1860–5). *jack/johnson*, 'rude' first black heavyweight boxing champion of the world (1908–15).

page 16

addis . . . actium . . . kumas: Ethiopia (1935), Egypt (31 BC), Ashanti (1902): Third World cities/forces overrun by Caesar.

babalawo: West African (Yoruba) priest.

o julia o baby g: fictive North American female type: blonde, helplessly voluptuous and usually sexually exploited . . . For '*julia*', see above, p. 113.

yabba (Twi *ayawa*): Afro-Caribbean earthenware vessel (bowl), used, like the calabash, in traditional kitchens. Just arrived in the *Oxford English Dictionary* (1986 Supplement).

accompong: Jamaica Maroon HQ since *c.* 1655.

tuntum achar eddoes: traditional Caribbean foods (ground-provisions).

pages 17–22

Hannibal . . . patton . . . rommel: conquistadores famous for their use of '*mo/bile armour*'.

seen?: Rasta for 'understood' (perhaps from civil service jargon).

highways littered with the red of dogs: in Nigeria, the Yoruba see Ogoun as, among other things, god of the highways, to whom are sacrificed, by motorists, hundreds of dogs each year. See Wole Soyinka's play, *The Road*.

these lookout crucifixions on the cliff: the most famous of these is perhaps Rio's 2,300 foot Corcovado, overlooking the celebrated Copacabana beach.

nkrumah's heedless statue: Kwame Nkrumah, Osageyfo of Ghana 1957–66, allowed statues erected in his own honour; he toppled, headless, in a military coup (the country's first) in 1966.

young caliban howling for his tongue: see Shakespeare's *The Tempest*. Caliban has become an anti-colonial/Third World symbol of cultural and linguistic revolt.

algonquin pontiac: N. Amerindian (Great Lakes) leader against the British (1763).

tupac amaru ii: Amerindian (Inca) rebel leader against the Spanish conquistadores 1780–1.

my heart at wounded knee: last battle stand of the Amerindian (Sioux) freedom fighters (against the USA) 1890.

tacky: Afro-Jamaican slave leader of the 1760 revolt.

man song (Mansong or Three Finger'd Jack): another Afro-Jamaican slave
rebel leader, Maroon & maverick.
These rebels, presaged in Dante's *Inferno* and already glimpsed in Michelangelo's paintings under the doom of the Sistine Chapel.

pages 23–7

Le jour est clair . . . : from the French medieval (eleventh-century) *Chanson de
Roland*.
london bridge is fall/en down: from the folk song/children's game/kaiso.
when joshua fit the battle of jericho: Negro spiritual.
ex-barbadian: not Barbados, my island, but El Barbade; both mean 'bearded'.
notre-dame de cap-henri: Henri Christophe of Haiti's cathedral, montaged
from Charlemagne's capital at '*aachen*'.
　　'*i will build cathedrals/now that i am king*' is from Derek Walcott's 1949
verse play, *Henri Christophe*. Both Charlemagne and Henri Christophe were
attempting post-imperial imperiums.
nodalbingians the widukind: Germanic tribes.
boniface: British-born (AD 680) Benedictine monk and evangelist to Charlemagne's Francia and to the Germanic 'heathens' beyond; murdered by them
in AD 754.
niggers niggers everywhere: in addition to the obvious meaning, reference to an
early negative Caribbean review of the author's *Rights of Passage* (1967).
naipaul of the middle passage: V. S. Naipaul, the Trinidad-born writer,
published a critique of the Caribbean in 1962, *The Middle Passage* (slave
trade passage from Africa to the Americas, and its consequences).
lord constantine: Trinidad-born Leary (Sir, later Lord) Constantine (?1900–
71), one of the most versatile of Caribbean cricketers, and certainly the most
highly imperially honoured. His 'elevation to the peerage' ('from Lords to the
Lords', 1969) was seen, in some quarters, as (nursery rhyme/kaiso) *london
bridge is fall/en down*.
i/ching. ken . . . *ch'eng h'siang*: from the *I Ching*, ancient Chinese Book of
Wisdom.

page 28

alcuin: Charlemagne's Master of the Schools, actually wrote this poem to the
cuckoo.

pages 29–30

anglo-saxon chronicle: eleventh–twelfth century English historical record from
oral tradition (see also '*dialect of the tribes*' in stanza above).
ga . . . *gar*: 'dark tribes'.

derek walcott's pitcher of clear metaphor: the St Lucia-born poet and play-wright has for a long time advocated in his verse, an H_2O_2 simplicity:

> I seek
> As climate seeks its style, to write
> Verse crisp as sand, clear as sunlight,
> Cold as the curled wave, ordinary
> As a tumbler of island water
> (from 'Islands', *Selected Poems* (1964), p. 45)

the portuguese will put her face up for sale: reference to the Virgin of Guadeloupe.

marinus of tyre: mid-second century AD mathematical geographer and founder of modern cartography (latitude/longitude); exploratory thinker preparing way for Ptolemy, Prince Henry the Navigator, and Columbus. First appears in Caribbean poetry in A. J. Seymour's (Guyana) *For Christopher Columbus*.

sycorax: Caliban's mother.

the black magnificenti/dei medici: the ?unbalanced montage world of the Mediterranean (Norse, Byzantine, Afro/European) produced Aesop, Alcmar, Socrates, Severus, Cleopat, Julia, Vercingetorix, Sycorax, Hannibal, Othello, Angelo Solimann Africanus and several of the Medicis.

> Bronzino's portrait of Alessandro [de' Medici] in the Uffizi Palace in Florence shows him with woolly hair and thick lips. Gino Capponi says: 'His mother was a mulatto slave and he had the dark skin, thick lips, and curly hair of a Negro.'
>
> Alessandro was not the only one of the Medicis to show a Negro strain. Cosimo III appears by his portrait to have been even more Negroid, while Cosimo's son, Gian Gastone, bears a striking resemblance to Dumas père. (For their pictures see C. H. Russell's *Regiae Familiae Mediceorum Etruriae*, pp. 18, 44.)
>
> Charles II of England was a Medici on his mother's side. G. F. Young (*The Medici* (1909)) says of him, 'His dark hair and swarthy complexion showed traces of Medici blood.'
>
> Catherine de' Medici, Queen of France, Alessandro's supposed sister, also had a son, the Duc d'Alençon, who was to all appearances a mulatto.

Extracts from J. A. Rogers, *World's Great Men of Color* (NY 1947/1972), Vol. 2, pp. 30–1.

pages 31–3

Here is the pivot of the Euro-imperialist/Christine mercantilist aspect of this book: '*the frozen first atomic bomb*'. Its creation of its own equilibrium creates disequilibriums elsewhere, one such being the '*sal/hara . . . sal/hell*'.

sa/hara: the world's greatest desert, origin of the *'harm/attan the harmattan'*, the dry drying seasonal climate-changing wind and starting point of much of my poetry since *Rights of Passage*. Since the mid 1960s, the Sahara has been undergoing one of its cyclical expansions, bringing drought and famine into much of Africa. Thousands have perished, from time to time in full view of (Western/Mont Blanc) TV and film crews. This has created, especially since *c.* 1983, an unusually West/Blanc people-artist humanitarian response: BAND AID, LIVE AID, SPORTS AID ('The Race against Time') and so on, the most impressive (most highly publicized) being the tremendous LIVE AID pop concerts and the US for AFRICA phono and video recording, *'We are the world'* (see 'Julia'), featuring a harmonious galaxy of singing stars and superstars, which has so far (May 1986) realized some US\$ 100 million in royalties.

sudan . . . bel uur (Ethiopia) *. . . niger*: some of the areas hardest hit by the famine/drought.

sa/hell (Sahel): S.W. Sahara; literally its hell.

pages 34–6

equiano . . . paul/robeson . . . othello the moor: celebrated blacks, not to be mistaken for the *'black faces'* *'miners of the empire'*. (A reference also to the role of Othello, seldom played by blacks, though there was Paul Robeson's awesome presentation, but by white actors in 'black face'.

Olaudah Equiano (?1745–?1801) was born near Igbo Onitsha, Nigeria; captured and sold as a slave to Barbados and Virginia and then as a maritime slave, based in England (1757), from where he worked (?cabin-boy) on a British naval vessel in the Mediterranean, and later on (?valet) a series of merchant ships which made several trips to the West Indies and N. America, taking the opportunity to trade for himself on the side, in order to earn and save enough money to purchase his freedom, which he achieved at Montserrat (his owner sailing with the ship) in 1766. He continued as a free black able bodied seaman and navigator for several years more, including an unsuccessful attempt on a northeast passage to India (1773) and an expedition to the Mosquito Shore of Honduras (1775) in his itinerary.

After his maritime phase and, it is said, his conversion to Calvinism (he'd always said that he was a predestinarian), he became completely caught up, not surprisingly, in the Humanitarian (Anti-Slavery) Movement. It was he who in 1783 called the attention of Granville Sharp to the massacre of +130 slaves on the good ship *Zong*, while still off the W. African coast; and in 1786, perhaps connected with this action, he was appointed Commissary for Stores for the Black Poor Being Shipped Off to Sierra Leone, but he lost this position, even before the project left England, because of a quarrel with its authorities.

In 1789 Equiano published his autobiography, *The interesting narrative of the life of Olaudah Equiano or Gustavus Vasa the African*; practically our only source of knowledge of this brother who, aged 12, taught himself to read and write his master's language; who, despite his 'navigation', never got back to Africa (even his request to go as a volunteer missionary was turned down); and who once had to *prove*(!) to certain English critics that he was in fact a 'pure African' and not, as they alleged, a saltwater nigger from (Danish) Santa Cruz in the West Indies.

In 1792 Equiano, who seems to have spent his last years in and/or near Cambridge and Cambridge University, was married 'to Miss [Susan] Cullen, daughter of Mr C of Ely, in same county'. St Andrew's Parish Church, Chesterton, has a cautionary memorial tablet to his multiracial daughter.

paul/robeson (1898–1976): one of the world's greatest concert singers in any class or colour and plutonic interpreter of the Negro Spiritual ('that unforgettable bass'), superb international actor and athlete, generous humanitarian and political and intellectual activist, 'the definitive Renaissance— and modern—Othello', like *jack/johnson* (black heavyweight champion of the world 1908–15), was not, to put it mildly, popular with the (US) Establishment, especially after he declared his Communist sympathy and affiliation in the 1950s. He was denied his American passport and effectively banned from public performance at home (and abroad) for the last rich twenty years of his life.

bhopal: in December 1984, Mont Blanc (US Union Carbide) exploded in this Central Indian city (memories of Nazi genocides of gas and of Hiroshima), maiming and destroying thousands.

pages 37–9

irie: Rasta for 'high', 'happy', though this poem is a version of Thomas of Celano's *irae* thirteenth-century Latin hymn.

my lai: infamous place and incident of Vietnam war, where all the villagers (all civilians) were slaughtered by US troops, 16 March 1968. See also *'Mai Village'*.

sharpeville: White S. African police massacre of scores of blacks protesting against racial discrimination, 21 March 1960.

ho chi (minh) (1890–1969): North Vietnamese revolutionary leader.

marti: Jose Marti (1853–95), ideologist/activist of the Cuban War of Independence, 1895–?98.

makandal: *vodoun* priest who played key role in events leading to the successful slave revolution in St Domingue/Haiti.

fedon: Grenada freedom fighter during the period of slavery.

sun yat sen (1866–1925): 'Father of the Chinese Republic'.

nyabingeh: a militant Rasta 'nation'.

guernica: ancient capital of the Basques, destroyed by aerial bombardment (1937) during the Spanish Civil War; cried out against by Picasso in a painting of that name.

che (guevara): handsome, bearded, beret-wearing icon of the Cuban Revolution.

nanny: early eighteenth-century Jamaica Maroon Queen Mother (*'nanny, nanahemmaa'*).

mahdi: Islamic (non-Q'ranic) concept and persona of redemption, leading to liberation (for a time) of the Sudan from Egyptian and British control (Khartoum) in the late nineteenth century.

long march: epic 8,000 mile trek (1934–5) of Chinese Communists under Mao Tse-tung, as strategic redeployment of forces during the Chinese Revolution.

bandung (Conference April 1955): first meeting of Third World/non-aligned leaders in the post-colonial world.

brimestone (Brimstone) *hill*: ancient Amerindian redoubt and settlement, later British fort, St Kitts, West Indies.

rodney (Walter): brilliant Guyanese/Caribbean intellectual and political activist, blown to bits in Georgetown in 1980.

ras makonnen: a Caribbean intellectual and political activist in Kenya during the Kenyatta (Mau Mau) war of liberation.

moncadas: it was the Moncada Barracks in Santiago de Cuba (symbol of the Batista Dictatorship) that Fidel Castro unsuccessfully attacked on 26 July 1953; making the date and place and incident a symbol of the later successful Revolution of 1959.

shaka: great Zulu military leader in confrontation with the British in S. Africa in the 1820s.

malan . . . verwoerd, vvoster, pik van botha: litany of racist S. African apartheid leaders.

herero: Namibian cattle people quatramated by the Germans after an uprising in 1907; see also 'Nam'.

seminole: Amerindian group in the Florida area, with Afro-American connections.

pages 40–7

tell your priests to foretell/that a white god falls down from heaven tomorrow: so-called Aztec presage of Cortez invasion, but also heard elsewhere.

amoy: one of the five Chinese ports forced open by The Video Tape Salesman to European trade (1842).

king kong: cultural gorilla of the Silent Screen.

blondie: the eternally young, sensible Mrs Middle America of the 'comic' strips.

pages 48–50

Sees the entry of the *sagres* (q.v., p. 115) expeditionary missiles (*'sticks rods roads bullets straight objects'*) into the 'target/circle' (*'round hut round village cooking pots'*) of W. Africa; in the same way that in 'Titan' missiles of the Spanish conquistadores enter into the '*cenote*' culture of the Amerindians.

oar prong put put: missiles. '*put put*' is a simple outboard engine.

kola nut: used especially in Muslim Africa as stimulant and (here) as token of greeting. Also, as '*bissi*' ('Stone') used by Caribbean Maroons as physick.

makola (market) *blue*: Yoruba dye, used in the decoration of cloth.

black hole of kaneshie: dark lagoon, Accra, Ghana.

odoum: ceiba, silk cotton tree; seat of spirits and the ancestors.

page 51

quetzalcoatl: Aztec serpent and rainbow god, icon, in this poem, of the New World; counterpoints with Kwa (Sudanic) sky-god 'Xango', who ends the book.

pages 53–54

In Port-au-Prince, Haiti, when I first visited in 1968–9, there was a great public mural by the artist Alexandre Wah, depicting the history of his country as a single, unfolding episode in montage: one image running into, echoing, continuing and extending another. This is the technique being attempted in this poem, dedicated here to Alexandre Wah.

cap: Cap Haitien, N. Haiti site of Henri Christophe's citadel. Charlemagne converses with Christophe about this in 'Song Charlemagne', earlier. Aimé Césaire in his *Cahier*, likened the citadel, one of the Seven Wonders of Our New World, to a ship of liberty fronting the Atlantic ('*itself still sailing where the islands float*'—('Citadel').

toussaint (L'Ouverture): leader of revolution in St Domingue/Haiti, seen here as *zemi* of the only successful large-scale slave rebellion in history.

zemi: Arawak/Amerindian representations in stone of divine/ancestral spirits. A characteristic of the zemi is the heavy brow and lidless eyes (see '*lidless legba l'ouverture*' in 'Salt'.

dessalines: one of Toussaint's successors.

la crete-a-pierrot: site of one of Dessalines' bloodiest ?victories.

pages 55–60

Angelo Solimann Africanus (c. 1721–76): 'friend, favourite, and tutor of European royalty. Personal attendant of Prince Lobkowitz and later of Prince de Lichtenstein. Still later, companion of Joseph II of Austria, with the approval of his mother, Empress Maria Theresa . . . Francis I, Emperor of the Holy Roman Empire, liked him so well that he invited him to enter his personal service. Abbé Gregoire . . . wrote a sketch of him in his *Litterature des Nègres* (1808) . . .' (J. A. Rogers, *World's Great Men of Color*, Vol. 2 (1947/1972), p. 551).

hounfour: *vodoun* place of worship/celebration.

mm . . . gigi . . . mata hari . . . caesarina borgia: well-known, beautiful, redoubtable, often dangerous women (*mm* is Marilyn Monroe).

head of grapes: one of the first sight/sees of Florence is the Piazza della Signoria and the cool Loggia dei Lanzi where stands a white, naked, callow youth, sword at half-rest (right hand); the left hand holding up and out before his face a head of grapes: Cellini's Perseus displaying not [*sir*] John the Baptist's head, but the Gorgon's; this, in the poem, is montaged montage with other representations of John's head on a platter.

barbers: Berber barbarians.

pyramid (of skulls): described (illustrated) in Mark Twain's *King Leopold's Soliloquy* (1906), an almost disappeared account of Belgian exploitation of the Congo by the author of *Huckleberry Finn*:

> Out of the skulls he will build a combined monument and mausoleum to me [Leopold] which shall exactly duplicate the Great Pyramid of Cheops, whose base covers thirteen acres, and whose apex is 451 feet above ground . . . He will build the pyramid in the center of a depopulated tract, a brooding solitude covered with weeds and the mouldering ruins of burned villages, where the spirits of the starved and murdered dead will voice their laments forever in the whispers of the wandering winds. . . . (p. 54)

bucky: buckra, backra, Ibo, Efik *mbakra*: (white) boss.

m16s: deadly ultra modern (1980s) automatic assault rifles, much in often casual use among paramilitary forces: civil, criminal, guerrilla.

three bags full. the local raw material of lies: echo of the folk rhyme, 'Ba ba black sheep'.

ring a round with roses of barb wire: another rhyme echo.

buttapan (butterpan): what 'Blanc' discards; industrial waste converted by Third World 'caliban' into something he/she can use; the best Caribbean example being the discarded Trinidad oil industry drums converted into steel drum pans, regarded as one of the genuinely new (certainly ingenious) musical instrument creations of the twentieth century.

In the Caribbean and no doubt elsewhere in the Third World, the *buttapan* is used as a (transportable) container for food and even for possessions. *Buttapan culcha* (there is a poem called this and about this by the Jamaican dub poet, Mutabaruka) is the peasant/poor man/*rasta*/*cultural gorilla* 'alternative', seen by satraps like Angelo as *dropout*.

sonny rollins: one of the great jazz saxophonists of the modern (post-bop) era. In the early 1960s he 'dropped out' of what he felt was becoming a musical rat-race and went into a kind of chromatic hibernation, discarding old clichés and exploring all alone new possibilities in his instrument high up in the winds/*spires* of the *brooklyn bridge* (New York). The result was his 1962 'breakthrough' LP, 'The Bridge'.

massacuriman: a S. American-Amerindian folklore spirit; kind of hydra headed, hence his Rasta/John the Baptist-like locks. Carl Abrahams' 'Columbus' (see cover) is a *massacuriman*.

magic lanthorn lilies: mystics often describe experiences connected with lilies. Miss Queenie, Kumina Queen of Jamaica, for instance, describes as part of her spirit world initiation into *kumina*, a Kikongo/Caribbean religious 'survival', how she was immured within the huge dark trunk of a silkcotton tree until the fortieth night when suddenly the darkness was illuminated by lilies: 'Seven lilies an is seven a dem blow . . .' And is the angel in Fra Angelico's painting 'The Annunciation', not presenting Mary with a lily . . . ?

obi . . . blue . . . susumba: Afro-Caribbean herbs and herbal medical (*obi*) terms.

back dam: area at back of Guyanese farm/land settlements; literally the land behind the dam.

lla lla llaaa illlllalla: Muslim call to prayer; 'there is one God, Allah (and Mohammet is his prophet)'.

malcolm (Malcolm X: Malcolm Little, El-Hajj Malik El-Shabazz; b. 1925, assassinated 1965): Black Muslim militant and ideologist of the Black Power (1960s/early '70s) period.

pages 61–4

guanahani coyoacan vera cruz: New World place names. Guanahani (San Salvador/Watlin Island, Bahamas), Columbus's first landfall in the Americas; Vera Cruz, seaport on the Spanish Main of Mexico and gateway, during the period of the Spanish American Empire, to Peru; Coyoacan, place of the *coyote*, on the Mexican plateau.

popocatepetl: Mexican volcano.

tetemextitan: a name of the capital of the Aztecs.

guatomec (Cuauhtemoc): Moctezuma's successor, Aztec freedom fighter against Titan/Cortez.

golden shrimp: royal Aztec decorative motif.

i will let them worship the head of my horse: Cortez thought (for some time, at least; until *guatomec*) that the Aztecs he was conquering were deifying, not defying, him. There is some evidence, though, that they were making icons of his horses—never seen before in the Americas. And he himself became identified with *akbal*, god of death and the underworld (see his 'descent' into my pictopoem of the temple of Akbal).

mol and moon and white and yucatan: Mayan divine forces.

the house of the dead landlord: the world of the dark was also the place of birth, being, bones, origins. Disease, disasters, death also came (escaped) from this Mictlan and it was the responsibility of the priests of this House to suck 'afflicting darkness' back down into the underworld. In the poem, Cortez is both searcher for bones and origins, and is himself the afflicting darkness (of conquest) being sucked (back) into the dark, so that he has to '*vomit out destroy destroy . . .*'.

akbal: club-footed (like Cortez) Aztec god of the underworld.

atahuallpa: Emperor of the Inca Empire (Peru), destroyed by Pizarro 'one sudden afternoon' November 1532.

darien: Titan/Cortez is here thinking of John Keats's poetic error in 'On first looking into Chapman's Homer', mistaking Balboa for Cortez:

> Then felt I like some watcher of the skies
> When a new planet swims into his ken;
> Or like stout Cortez when with eagle eyes
> He star'd at the Pacific—and all his men
> Look'd at each other with a wild surmise—
> Silent, upon a peak in Darien.

pages 65–8

the cards smelled of the gun/man ... jesus christ was the hanged man of industrial/birmingham ... by the waters: echoes of T. S. Eliot's *The Waste Land*.

ebony & ivory: New World plantations brought together black (ebony) and white (ivory) in an unplanned and generally (especially by the 'superior' whites) disapproved interculturation; echoed (more generously, glamorously) in the pop-song duet video/recording of the same name by Stevie Wonder (Ebony) and the former-Beatle Paul McCartney (Ivory) with decor of black and white pianos.

shiloh shennandoa O/black/hole of calcutta: plantation place names/battles/songs/spirituals/events: US South and (Calcutta) India.

harddough bread: Jamaican description of 'hard', 'tight', close-textured, 'poor people', 'buttapan culture' bread.

gary sobers: world's greatest all-round cricketer; Bajan-born panther and *pythagoras* of cricket.

stoned me into silence on my stony/hill: in 1983, Michael Smith, young brilliant Jamaican dub (US ?rap) poet, was stoned to death by assailants not yet brought to book, for apparently heckling a Government politician during a meeting at/on Stony Hill, suburb of Kingston, the capital.

miss universe ... not the only virgin mary: in 1983, the first ever black to become Miss America, had her title taken away when it was disclothed through certain pictures in a popular glossy magazine that she was apparently not born under Virgo.

sound systems: batteries of huge loudspeakers, capable of volcanic outpouring, used at dances and even some parties and public events where popular music is required; developed in Jamaica as aspect of the development of Jamaican popular music from the ska and rock steady of the '60s, the reggae and DJ trackings since. And so, a series of musical references: *wired for sound, disco brams, eel/ectronic micro/maniacs, wayside preachers' harps.* 'get/up stand/up stand/up for [your] rights', is a *bob/marley* theme song. The reference to *cornmeal porridge* is from Marley's 'No woman no cry'; '*i see the towers*

125

rising' echoes Bob Andy's 'Fire Burning' from his Kingston 1975 LP 'The music inside me'; while '*by the waters*' [of babylon] is specifically here from a Rasta chant.

page 69

sauteurs [see note on 'Nix', p. 115] *maggotty six mens bay*: small picturesque backwater Caribbean places.

jean rhys hummingbirds of coulibri decay: Jean Rhys (1894–1979), the Caribbean (Dominica) born writer, gave us, in her last novel, *Wide Sargasso Sea* (1966) a bitter-sweet account of the *tristes tropiques* and their European consequences. The novel is a variation of *Jane Eyre* and begins in the Dominica Great House, Coulibri; which, as *colibri*, means hummingbird.

pages 70–2

texcoco tenochtitlan: Aztec place names; pre-Aztec and Aztec capitals on same site, Lake Texcoco (drained away by the Spaniards!) in the 'Valley of Mexico', on which Mexico City (*tenochtitlan*) now stands.

pages 73–9

> In June 1976 South Africa's black townships burst out in the most serious racial violence since the creation of the Union. It began in the huge Soweto (south-western townships) agglomerated near Johannesburg, with a protest by school children against the imposition of Afrikaans as the medium of instruction. It soon spread not only to other African townships around the Rand and Pretoria, but also to Natal and the Cape, involving Indian and Coloured youths as well as Africans. Repeatedly apparently suppressed, it as repeatedly flared up again [and again] throughout the year ... and expressed a massive radicalization of black youth ... (*Southern Africa Encyclopedia 1984–85*), p. 750.

This lament for the hundreds of Soweto children slaughtered and wounded by the S. African security forces, and the thousands of *herero* massacred by the Germans in *Nam*ibia at the turn of the century, follows the vulture/condor from Tetemextitan to the Cape of Good Hope (!) and across the veldt up the Rift Valley, past the *maasai* and *kilimanjaro* and *the lakes of the luo* as far north as Ethiopia (*ityopia*).

The Xosa words of the lament were given to me by Nomtuse Bata Mbere of Azania/Botswana, to whom I would like to dedicate this version of the poem ...

Place names include: *namibia* (S.W. Africa), *azania* (Black S. African name for their country); *zimbabwe* (ancient African empire, name adopted by independent S. Rhodesia); *kinshasa* (formerly Leopoldville, capital of the

Republic of Zaire); *ityopia* (Ethiopia); *limpopo*, river that marks (northern) boundary of S. Africa with the (Black) 'frontline' states; seen here as gateway (*legba* the *limper*).

Nation/language groups include: *basuto, zulu, maasai, herero, kikuyu, swahili, luo.*

People names include (Black leaders) *mokhethi* (Soweto) *shaka, kenyatta* and *kimathi* (Mau Mau/Kenya freedom fighters and (Kenyatta) first President of Kenya); *patrice* Lumumba (1925–61, murdered Congo/Zaire Independence fighter and (for eleven weeks) first Prime Minister of Congo Republic); *nzinga*, Warrior Queen of Mbundu, Congo (1582–1663), famous for resistance campaigns against the Portuguese in the 1620s. Whites: *malan* (1874–1959), Nationalist (Apart/hate) PM 1948–54; name used, with *malam*, as warning bell in this poem.

Other words of interest: *nim* (tree), *noom* (fatal noon), *nam* (soul), *streggaed* (stripped with a sound like reggae guitar strings); *manyatta* (Maasai habitation); *bantustan* (S. African reservation for Africans; 'homelands': homeless African homelands).

Nam (the title of the poem and word used throughout the work) means not only *soul*/atom but *indestructible self/sense of culture under crisis*. Its meaning involves root words from many cultures (meaning 'soul'; but also (for me) *man* in disguise (*man* spelled backwards)); and the *main* or *mane* of *name* after the weak *e* or tail has been eaten by the conquistador; leaving life (*a*/alpha) protected by the boulder consonants *n* and *m*. In its future, *nam* is capable of atomic explosion: *nam . . . dynamo . . . dynamite* and apotheosis: *nam . . . nyam . . . onyame . . .*

pages 80–7

sheena: China.

prospero: Shakespeare's plantation owner in *The Tempest* (see also *caliban* note p. 116); 'the man who possesses us all' of *Mother Poem*.

jackie robb/inson r. t-d2: N. American entertainers (baseball, a film robot/*star wars*) connected with the expression 'before I could say Jack Robinson'.

star/trick [trek] . . . star wars: space age TV/films on the verge of magical reality.

pascal & co/balt: ?French philosophers who developed computer (and ?nuclear) *linguage*.

charlie chap . . . bo/jangles: Charlie Chaplin, famous star of Silent Screen; Bill Robinson, brilliant black dancer and underground/submerged teacher and choreographer of many (more famous) in the Fred Astaire/Shirley Temple era.

chauncery lane: not the London walkway, but downtown Kingston (Jamaica) reggae-making and recording centre.

sputnik: Earth's first (1957 Soviet) spacecraft, with its characteristic transmitted *bleeps.*

curser: tongue of the computer.

since menelek was a bwoy: ?inexplicable Bajan expression='for ages', 'for as
long as I can remember'. Menelek I (1000 BC), son of Solomon and Sheba, is
traditionally regarded as founder of the Ethiopian royal line, one of the oldest
in world history. Menelek II defeated the Italians at the Battle of Aduwa in
1896, to preserve Ethiopia's ancient independence.

brigg/flatts: nation language (*jordie*) long poem by Basil Bunting, British
(Northumbrian) poet (1900–85).

hervokitz: M. J. Herskovits, cultural anthropologist, whose *Life in a Haitian
valley* (1937), *The myth of the negro past* (1941), etc. redress the notion that
Blacks in Africa and the New World have (had) no culture.

de pisan cantos: Ezra Pound's eccentric long poem about cultural distress . . .

ink.le & yarico: seventeenth-century Caribbean tale of ill-starred love of Carib
daughter (Inkle) for a shipwrecked European opportunist.

anglo sax/on chronicle: Early English records of English history from beginning
of Christian era until twelfth century.

pages 88–91

Twoom, or *room*, becomes *tomb*.

X/self visits one of those modern 'Installation' art exhibitions (in Kingston,
Jamaica) and contrasts its wasteful Byzantine poverty of opulence (still/life)
with the opulence of poverty (still life) in the world outside.

belly/woman: pregnant woman.

for/nicalia: inverted version of California?

nine miles of black star liners: reference to popular song about Marcus Garvey
who, in the 1920s and '30s tried, among many other sisyphean upliftments,
to create a transatlantic fleet of ships (from the Americas to Africa) in
countervail to, say, the Cunard White Star liners.

red gal ring . . . caymanas: places in Kingston, Jamaica.

no mcarthur on the deck of aircraftcarrier nimitz: Nimitz was not the name
of the carrier, but the photograph of General Douglas McArthur of the
victorious US Armed Forces receiving the formal surrender of Japan from
Emperor Hirohito on board the USS *Missouri* is one of the visual classics of
our time (comparable to the earlier 'Sea come no further' or 'When did you
last see your father' or 'Nelson dying at Trafalgar').

The other, more recent picture, is of 'the peoples liberation army' (Grenada)
surrendering to US Marines, 28 October 1983 ('*the portuguese/have beaten
us . . . at their own game*'—see 'Stone').

pages 93–5

we draw the lion/line: mark and symbol of pride and resistance: Ethiopia,
Rasta, E. African *simba*.

lome . . . abidjan: W. African cities.

janga (W. African *njanga*): river prawn.

the portuguese/have beaten us at last: refers to the defeat of the Brazilian Maroon Republic of Palmares in 1696 after some ninety years of independence:

> At its height, the town of Palmares is said to have had a population of about 20,000 [African/Brazilian ex-slaves], with a hinterland which gave a total fighting force of some 10,000 men [and women]. Because of the increasing danger to white settlements, the Portuguese in 1696 assembled an army of nearly 7000 men for the attack. Palmares was [protected] by a stockade, but lacked the artillery necessary for defense, and was finally taken. Most of the warriors committed suicide, and those who were captured, being deemed too dangerous to be reenslaved, were killed . . .
>
> M. J. Herskovitz, *The myth of the negro past* (1941/1958), p. 91.

vieques porto bello choc guantanamo: Caribbean harbours, some used as US naval bases.

nanny nanahemmaa: Nanny (b. ?1683), warrior/Queen (Mother) (nanahemmaa) of the E. Jamaica Maroons (*c*. 1730–?50), led successful ten year struggle for independence from British plantations, guaranteed in a Peace Treaty of 1740. She came from the great W. African *ohemmaa* tradition, wherein certain Queen Mothers, at points of crisis, had the authority (and ability) to seize power and carry through the necessary political (and military) functions of the state.

matapee: S. American (Guyana) Amerindian elongated basket, usually suspended from ceiling, for straining cassava juice.

callaloo: S. Amerindian word for a kind of spinach and more generally for edible green leaves.

olodumare yam: yam, in Africa, and to some extent in the African New World/Caribbean (especially among Maroons), is regarded as a plant/food specially connected with the gods. Olodumare is the Yoruba Supreme God. See also *'the yams of ibadan'* ('Ice/Nya') and *'olodumare's conflagration'* ('Sunsong').

runagate: refrain taken from the Afro-American Robert E. Hayden's poem of that name; best *heard* on the LP 'Roses & Revolutions' (Washington, DC 1975), performed by Roscoe Lee Browne and Ruby Dee.

square/foot dog: *akbal* of the poem *Titan*; Aztec Cerberus . . .

solares bolivare palanquin: S. American freedom fighters; the last a Maroon.

pages 96–8

kaieteur: one of the world's greatest waterfalls ('opposite' Niagara) in the Guyana hinterland.

rock/steady: early (Jamaican) reggae form.

cesaire: Aimé Césaire, b. 1913 in the French Caribbean island of Martinique. His fabulous long poem *Cahier d'un retour au pays natal* (1939) evolved the concept of *negritude*: that there is a black Caliban Maroon world with its own aesthetics (*sycorax*), contributing to world and Third World consciousness.

pages 99–101

yemajaa: W. African/Afro Caribbean and Afro Brazilian goddess of the waves, of the salt waters, of the Middle Passage.

charcoal from the castries mountain: Castries, seaport and capital of St Lucia, was a coaling station (1878–c. 1948).

cashew seagrape fatpork macca quickstick/palm . . . coconut: seashore ('*salt fruit*') and/or dry (sand soil) plants; gifts to yemajaa.

maljo: evil eye; anti-life magic.

sipple: slip, to slip away, slippery.

pages 102–5

ankh: Ancient Egyptian symbol of life in the form of a looped cross.

kilimanjaro: African twin (snow capped '*holy mountain*' on the equator) and opposite of/to 'Mont Blanc' (q.v.) and in dis/equilibrium with it. As Blanc rises, Kili '*widens deepens darkens*' becoming '*wound whole/absence* . . .'

steel pan bands: Trinidad *buttapan* invention of musical pans from ?discarded (oil industry) steel drums.

the old man with his . . . bag: Uncle Macoute (Bag), Papa Bois, Legba.

rodney: not now the murdered black militant of 'Dies irie', but the English eighteenth-century Admiral commemorated in a Roman toga in Spanish Town Square, Jamaica.

nelson: a statue of Lord Nelson, with iconographic one hand (the other lost in battle) was out here in the Caribbean (Barbados, in fact) even before the far taller one in Trafalgar Square, London.

illimani arequipa coropuna yerupaja cotopaxi [nevada del] *ruiz*: Andean volcanoes.

pages 107–11

Xango: Pan African god of thunder, lightning, electricity and its energy, sound systems, the locomotive engine and its music; a great horseman. Appears also as Shango.

erzulie: Fon (Dahomey)/Haitian goddess of love and fertility.

de soto francisco coronado: Spanish conquistadores, explorers.

john/ford: N. American film director, especially of classic Westerns.

j/p morgan: nineteenth-century US entrepreneur, banker and multibillionaire.

high life: popular W. African musical and dance hall form.

abomey: ancient capital of Dahomey, famous for carved terracotta figures.

twists . . . bop hard bop soul bop funk: N. American jazz, gospel and pop dance forms.

new thing . . . soul rock skank: N. American and Jamaican (reggae) dance/ music forms; all Xango musics.

marley: Bob Marley (1945–81), Jamaican Rasta poet and reggae superstar and icon.

bunk johnson (1899–1949): legendary New Orleans jazz trumpeter.

There was a time in Barbados when Bajans, immune
from the tremours of the North Atlantic, cleaved
themselves into two main tribes. Those who practiced
Banja, and those who did not

The non-Bajan people fraid Banja, so much so that
Banja was not to be heard or seen on Sundays or any
other sacred day of the Lord

Banja could only hold sway iffing it was
a bank holiday or Saturday

Banja ent do nutten. Banja is just Banja. Banja get
ban a long time ago and get put in court and get
law pass and every-body tink Banja dead

Banja cut and thrive. Banja stay low and hide and
duck and weave

And Banja survive

Elton Elombe Mottley, *When Banja play, Bajan come*